Lumpy Porridge

and Other

Scottish Memories

Other books by Joyce Milne D'Auria

My Blood Is Royal
Billy Boy
Bridge Across Time (2016)

Lumpy Porridge

and Other

Scottish Memories

Joyce Milne D'Auria

Revised Edition
2015

Copyright 2010 by Joyce Milne D'Auria

All rights reserved. No part of this book may be reproduced in any form or by any electronic or mechanical means, including information storage and retrieval systems, without written consent from the author, except by a print reviewer, quoting brief excerpts.

Prepared for publication through
CreateSpace
by
Arucadi Enterprises, LLC
St. Petersburg, FL

Photos supplied by the author

Cover Design
theMurmaid™

ISBN: 1516944860
ISBN 13: 978-1516944866

DEDICATED TO

My wee brother, Robert (Bob Milne),
in Brisbane, Australia

TABLE OF CONTENTS

Foreword	ix
Adventures of a Recent Immigrant	1
Forget Black Puddin' c, 1960	1
Get Your Kicks on Route 66	5
A Scot in America	13
Waste Not, Want Not	13
By Yon Bonnie Banks	17
Mother's Day Memories	23
Old Friends Are the Best	31
My Husband and the Blonde	37
A Childhood in Lanarkshire	43
Kisses on the Bottom	43
The Glesca' Fair	49
Going for the Messages	55
Take Yer Lumps	59
Thruppence Worth, Please	63
The Joy-ce of Cooking	67
Upstairs on the Double	71

Travelling Back in Time	77
Say Wha'?	77
The Hazards of Driving in Scotland	81
Rainstorming	87
Brave Hearts Are not Worn on the Sleeve	91
The Hazards of Scottish Food	97
Going Home	101
Tall Tales My Grandfather Told Us	107
Sunday at Grandpa's	107
Showdown at the Big Tree Bar	111
The Scottish National Party: Hogmanay	119
Hogmanay: A Scottish New Year	119
My First Hogmanay	123
New Year Resolutions	127
New Year in a Highland Croft – 1860	131
About the Author	143
Acknowledgments	145

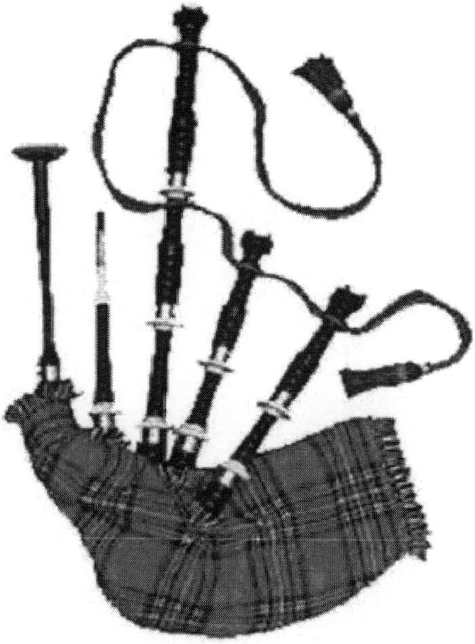

FOREWORD

Lumpy Porridge is a collection of reminiscences from this Scot who has lived in America for most of her adult life. Being Scottish is still a big part of me. Sometimes a word will pop out of my mouth that is not actually English but from the dialect we used in and around Glasgow. The words and sayings I grew up with are rich in expressive inferences, words that are onomatopoetic or, simply put, words that sound like what they mean.

Scottish people love a story, and I grew up listening to my grandparents' yarns, told in rich dialect. Many of the stories are based on their sometimes faulty and always colourful memories. Their humour, understated and focused on their own foibles takes a minute or two to sink in and leaves you walking away laughing.

Scots love to sing the old songs. All my life I have been a singer and always included Scottish songs in my repertoire.

Go to my website www.joycethescottishwriter.com for my recording of "My Ain Folk."

And my favourite poet is Robert Burns, of course.

This story writing started as the occasional contribution to a Scottish newspaper. The first was "Rainstorming," a story about the ubiquitous topic of weather conversations. And once I got my feet wet, so to speak, topics were flooding my mind on a regular basis until I realized there was quite a collection and it was time to go to print and reach a wider audience.

The original pieces had a special appeal to expats, and the stories reached them all over the world, one at a time. I loved their letters. Now they can read them anytime in this edition of *Lumpy Porridge* (with a couple of new stories added).

Please enjoy *Lumpy Porridge and other Scottish Memories* and contact me at www.joycethescottishwriter.com to leave a note or comment.

*RMS Mauritania of the Cunard line
leaving New York Harbour
after it dropped the author off c.1960.
That's her waving from the Empire State building!*

Adventures of a Recent Immigrant

Forget Black Puddin' c. 1960

The farewells in Glasgow; the fantastic ocean liner; the friends and family I had left behind faded, for the moment, from my mind as I looked, awestruck at the Statue of Liberty.

I arrived in New York City from Scotland with altogether too much luggage. No problem. The fatherly agent at the wharf where I disembarked from the trans-Atlantic liner Mauritania took a look at my crates of wedding gifts and household items and the tea chests packed full of my "wedding china" and clued me in. "If anyone asks you, tell them you've been married a year." I guess it had to do with paying, or in this case not paying, duty.

Before I continued my voyage westward, a fellow passenger invited me to the famous Oyster Bar for lunch. I was hesitant.

She coaxed me, "Never had 'em? You'll love 'em."

I discovered that I hate oysters. She was practically orgiastic over the slimy, slippery creatures.

That was yesterday, my first day in these Yoonided States. I learned quickly that nobody understands me unless I speak slowly.

Today the kind oyster lady and I travel by rail together

as far as Syracuse where she alights with a motherly backward glance. I can't imagine why she's concerned; I am a grown-up. Soon I'll be twenty, and for me this is all an enormous adventure.

Destination: Flint, Michigan, and my new husband's idea of a honeymoon cottage—an unfurnished upstairs apartment adjacent to the General Motors parking lot. We don't need a clock. The change of shifts defines morning, afternoon and night.

The train ride to Michigan from New York was very exciting, but here's one memory that has stayed clearly in my mind for decades:

It is morning and he has gone to work in our only car. Not that I'd risk driving on the wrong side of the road. I am still on Greenwich Mean Time and very hungry. A quick search of the ancient refrigerator reveals a can of Donald Duck orange juice and a shelf of Stroh's beer.

I'll have to immediately unpack something appropriate to wear and start walking to the nearest restaurant if I want to eat breakfast before they start serving lunch.

Sunday morning calls for dressy clothes—and a hat, I think. My suit is only slightly crushed; the blue and black brocade material tends to disguise that problem. Luckily my navy high-heeled shoes and the pillbox hat (very Jackie Kennedy), which completes the outfit to perfection, are easily retrieved from the suitcase. I wonder if the half-veil is overdoing it a bit, but I'm not going to spoil a beautiful velvet creation by dismantling it. I push it up on top of the hat to make it less conspicuous.

Ninety degrees in July is new to me. It never gets much above seventy in Scotland. I have never before had the experience of my spiked heels sinking into tarmac. I am brought to a halt every few steps and obliged to extricate my heel. It is slow going and I may have to walk farther. Not too many restaurants or teashops in this part of town. Just when the perspiration is beginning to stain my best clothes and dampen my sense of adventure, I see Sally's Diner. The red neon sign is flashing "Open" and the smell, oh! The smell is tantalizing. I am imagining ham and eggs, maybe some potato scones or rolls, and a big pot of tea.

The tables are full. No one is dressed for Sunday. Mostly workmen from the factory. They are looking at me—all of them. I guess men are the same the world over. I straighten my hat self-consciously and try to ignore them. There is one vacant yellow, plastic seat at the counter.

A very large woman comes out of the kitchen wielding a spatula and wiping it on the side of her dirty white apron. She opens her eyes wide, then squints at me and says one long word that I don't understand. Sounds like "Whaddayawan?"

I smile in return. "Could I have a menu, please?

She looks at a young fellow in the closest booth with her lip curled and one eyebrow cocked in a questioning expression. He shrugs and grins. She turns her stare towards me as though I've insulted her or I'm speaking in a foreign language, for goodness sake, and retreats to the kitchen. I hear words I've heard only in X-rated films, over the clatter of pots and pans.

I check my watch. Fifteen minutes I've waited. I cough to cover the unladylike sound of my stomach rumbling. A few minutes later she appears, sweating profusely, and slaps down a yellowed sheet of paper with menu items on it and splats of dead flies indicating its double use as a swatter.

I choose ham and two eggs and toast and tea. I look for marmalade on the counter. Maybe they don't have any.

"Dyawanemsunnyside or ov'reasy?"

I agree that it is sunny out. She sighs, shrugs, and ambles into the kitchen. I hope I have successfully placed my order because I am now extremely hungry and not a little embarrassed at being the centre of attention for reasons I can barely fathom.

LUMPY PORRIDGE

It takes her less time to cook the food than it did to find the menu. She reappears in five minutes with an enormous platter overflowing with a thick cut of meat, which they call ham here, and two eggs barely cooked, and brownish water with ice floating in it. My cuppa tea got lost somehow in the translation. I'll try again. "Coffee, please. I take it white." She slaps herself on the forehead and brings me black coffee. Fortunately there is a pitcher of cream on the counter.

I put the veil back on top of my hat out of my way and get busy finishing all that I find edible on the plate. There's been a slight misunderstanding here—but, I have learned something, and I hate to admit it, but coffee for breakfast is all right. In fact, I prefer it.

Is that why they call this "The Melting Pot?"

"Whadyatink?"

Mum's Fry-up
The Big Scottish Breakfast ~ Ham and Eggs and more.

In a large, larded iron skillet, fry slices of Ayrshire bacon and Lorne sausages.
Add black pudding and white (fruit pudding) till browned.
Remove to warmed platter.
Fry eggs, tattie scones, and tomato halves.
Optional additions: Mushrooms, baked beans, leftover potatoes fried
And fried bread (for the fearless)
Serve with a pot of tea, buttered toast, and marmalade.
Oatcakes may also be served.

Warning: When indulging in the big Scottish Breakfast it is not (I repeat NOT) recommended to start the meal off with the hostess's homemade porridge.

Get Your Kicks on Route 66

We weren't trying to make history. But perhaps we did create a footnote to history. Four intrepid Scots: two doctors, Hugh and Colin, and two nurses, Joyce and Mhairi, all fairly "fresh off the boat," left Flint, Michigan, in the early sixties on an adventure across America with high hopes and empty pockets.

Taking the legendary Route 66 from Chicago we followed it all the way to California. Scots ... On the Road. In this saga, we four immigrants from Fife, Motherwell, Coatbridge and Stornoway were on an adventure across the Yoonided States on the famous Route 66, and riding in style. The shiny blue and white '58 Edsel was only two years old.

It was a huge escapade, no doubt dreamed up one evening over a bottle of Glayva. In this tale of youthful exploration only the first names are used in order to protect the innocent. Though, come to think of it, we were all pretty innocent back then. Young, naïve, eager for adventure, fearlessly driving this enormous vehicle at speeds of up to 90 mph. (I didn't even look at the speedometer when the guys were driving.)

Years later Mhairi said, "We were so young and Scottish and new to everything, but just picturing you behind the wheel of that huge car, and trusting that we would arrive safely at our destination makes me quiver."

Six-foot-four Colin could spread out in the back seat and sleep while the three of us sat comfortably in the front. Of course, Mhairi and I were size sixes at the time. The Horizon Blue '58 Edsel with white trim went from 0 to 60 MPH in 10.2 seconds. It was obscenely roomy and gas guzzling and luxurious; some people thought it even looked obscene. It had been a bargain for reasons that quite escaped the eager Scottish car shopper.

Get your kicks on Roo-oote 66

By the time we reached Chicago we were into the swing of it, ready to hit "The Mother Road." Ready to get our kicks on Rte 66. The melody and the words of Bobby Troup's Route 66 was the backdrop for this trip. We sang the song and recognized all the places mentioned.

We left the Great Lakes behind and entered America's heartland. Going through Illinois (we pronounced it "Il-a-noise") we grew impatient with the already familiar industrial towns. We had a long way to go. In fact, more than 2,000 miles according to the song.

For the first few days we couldn't grasp the immensity of the distance. We had been raised in a country that was about a hundred miles across and three hundred miles long, give or take a few bens, glens, lochs an' wee back roads. In Missouri, we slowed down for a twisty road that crossed an iron bridge over the Big Piney River and stopped for big juicy steak and chips ("french fries" was not in our vocabulary) at The Devil's Elbow Café, then drove on. Tired from our long day, we were attracted to the VACANCY sign blinking at the Twin Six Motel. Our established routine was that one of the guys haggled over the price. We watched from the car while the bewhiskered owner, barely visible through a cloud of cigarette smoke, observed us from the "office" window. Our negotiator returned with the deal: Two rooms for $18 each. We had learned earlier that buying the two-room package was a real bargaining tool. Not that we were being stingy. We really had very little money. Lotsa potential ... no cash.

Next morning early, we were on the road. We hungry young women watched for a likely spot to have our usual hearty breakfast. One of the men must have been driving while we were half asleep for when we paid attention, it was already lunchtime. A huge flashing neon EAT sign invited us to feast at the Okie Steak House and Bar-B-Q. We had all developed a taste for hamburgers and, in the days before fast food, they were often huge and piled with Pappy's homemade sauce ... more chips.

Somehow we'd skipped right through Kansas (Route 66 barely dips into that state). But we did see a lot of Oklahoma. They are very proud of Route 66 there, and the double sixes signs were easy to follow.

Next we needed to stop at the Texaco stations with the big red star. "Gas War-Reg. 22," the sign read. And it meant cents! Bargain petrol was essential. Using Premium gasoline, we were supposed to get 12.5 MPG, but that was if you maintained 70 MPH or less. There were no statistics for travelling faster than that!

Texas, here we come. The two Scotsmen had to have ten-gallon hats. I forget where they bought them. It might have been when we stopped to see "25 Cages of Live Snakes" or perhaps it was at the museum where the mummy of an Indian girl, still clutching her baby two hundred years later, was the main attraction. Maybe it was in Amarillo where I was amazed to see that the only paved road was the one we were travelling. We got out of the car to explore and discovered red dirt roads just behind the stores. And me in high heels. Jings!

We were at the halfway point of our journey now. The intrepid Scottish travellers, somewhere in the Texas panhandle, were still following the double six signs, headed for California. The land coming into view was the stuff of Western Movies. Wide spacious grass plains, home to oil wells dipping toward the ground in slow motion like giant praying mantises hunting for insects. Huge oil derricks dotted the farmland in Texas, and the great monuments towering over towns were tall vessels of petrochemical refineries.

We cruised past a chain gang of prisoners repairing the ditch that lined the road, a painful reminder that not everyone had the high hopes for their future that buoyed us.

The big land boat cruised down Route 66 and we sang the blues along with the car radio and Frankie Laine singing about the moon and the stars and crying over lost love.

When we stopped at a drive-in, a girl with a red cowboy hat and a short skirt almost made the guys forget to order their usual hamburgers. The loudspeaker blared Marty Robbins' sad ballad of a gun battle in "Rosie's Cantina."

We went on a hunt for Rosie's Cantina but abandoned our fruitless search since we were nowhere near West Texas, and I think it might be a fictional place in any case. We'd crossed the state line into New Mexico by now, so we stopped and tried Mexican food (the Mexican mince was a wee bit too spicy) before spending the night at the Westward Ho motel.

At Kingman, Arizona, the sign pointing south said "Phoenix 184 miles" and pointing east said "Chicago 1235 miles." We'd come all that way and even farther. And pointing west to our destination it read, "Los Angeles" where Hugh's sister, an American for many long years, awaited a visit from her long-lost brother and his buddies. But the sign pointing northwest that informed him "Las Vegas 104 miles" caught the imagination of her wayward brother and the easily led cohorts, poker players all.

"We might never get another opportunity to see Las Vegas."

"It's kind of off our route. Do we have the time?"

"Och, jist one night, and we'll make up the time on the road."

"I'm definitely not going to spend much money."

"I'll just take $20 in ... well, maybe $30."

It was a short strategy meeting that ended in a unanimous decision.

"Let's go to Las Vegas."

We continued at 90 MPH, focused now on cleaning up in Vegas. Getting rich quick!

We were too young to be concerned about how we would survive tomorrow's journey through the desert after a night on the town.

It was late, maybe ten in the evening, when we negotiated our bargain motel and started to put on our party duds.

"Och, if you women don't stop plowterin' around and get in the car, everything will be closed." It was Colin in his suit and tie with his new ten-gallon hand at a jaunty 'Las Vegas' angle. Hugh was in the Edsel revving the motor.

Mhairi and I were still working on hair styling (curling for her; straightening for me). We still had eye shadow, mascara and lipstick to do and dresses not yet decided on.

I don't really know how we all survived that trip.

We sent the men off to find out when the casinos closed

and very soon they returned a wee bit red-faced. The cab driver had laughed at them.

"Man, they never close." Cab drivers get to see and hear everything. Can't you hear him telling his wife, "You should've seen the two Scotsmen in the cowboy hats, middle of the afternoon and they're worried about the casinos bein' closed ... they did speak Amurican pretty good, though."

We got as far as the Golden Nugget, and Mhairi and I got separated from the men, who had gone off to do some serious gambling with their $20 (or was it $30?). They never did confess to the extent of their extravagance.

Now here's a tale of Scottish thrift that would make yer granny proud:

Mhairi and I were on about our third free Drambuie when she hit the jackpot on the nickel machine. The payout of $8 went right into her purse; she snapped it shut and never opened it again till we were clear of Las Vegas.

Granny wouldna' have been quite sae proud of her fine Scottish sons though, who lost all of their $20 (or more likely $30). They appeared a couple of hours later skint, fu' of free booze and wailing about their bad luck. As we left the casino, people were alarmed and talking among themselves about the Scottish cowboys who'd lost "all their money." It is not unheard of for this kind of scenario to end up in suicide in Vegas. In this instance the biggest disaster was simply a bad Nevada hangover. And we were off, across the Saguaro-covered desert, to Los Angeles and on to San Diego to meet Hugh's hospitable sister, who gave us a fine Scottish/American welcome in San Diego.

Our Route 66 journey going West was a successful adventure.

After our visit, we found our way back East, and this time we remembered to give Las Vegas a wide berth.

*Scottish Cowboys and
the Gals They Lassoed*

Reader, get yourself a copy of this great social commentary poem. Robert Burns was astute politically, and ahead of his time.

The Twa Dugs

Caesar
    I see how folk live that hae riches;
    But surely poor folk maun be wretches.

Luath (responds)
    They're no' say wretched's ane wad think, …

    Love blinks, Wit slaps, and social Mirth
    Forgets there's Care upo' the earth.

… Robert Burns

A Scot in America

Waste Not, Want Not

Musings on the Scottish reputation for being thrifty

When I was a wee lassie in Lanarkshire we were taught three things: Piety, Thrift, and Wheesht. (I remember "Wheesht" was sort of like "Hush" but with the authority of a Scottish Mum.) Oh, and Telling the Truth. That was definitely required. Roughly translated, piety meant that you went to the Kirk all day on the Sabbath; you got a shilling a week, and sixpence was supposed to go in the collection plate; you were expected to be seen and not heard. About the truth part … to tell you the truth, I never thought too highly of Piety, Thrift, and Wheesht. I thought it was an over-rated formula for raising weans. But that's jist me, mind ye!

If you were brought up the same way, you may find it interesting to speculate on how many of those childhood messages still whirl and wheech around in your brain and influence your daily decisions.

I'd like to talk about the thrift myth. Caution and good sense should not be confused with lack of generosity. Yes! We made do, but we never really did without and there was always enough to share. What a great lesson that was. "Reduce, Reuse, Recycle," the mantra of the environmentalist, just makes good sense.

The Co-op horse-drawn cart brought six pints of milk (and picked up the empty bottles) each morning. Old Monty, the Clydesdale horse, left his calling card, not just once in a while, but every single day for years. Good old Monty ... probably got his moniker from Field Marshall Montgomery, a hero in our childhood. Every day there was a large mound of manure outside our gate.

I'll never figure out how my father trained that horse. Dad went out with the shovel and brought that precious fertilizer into the back yard to nourish his rose garden. At one point I counted two hundred rose bushes out there. It was a spectacular display of colour. To this day the fragrance of roses brings back memories of my father, the crazy paving paths he built and myriad species of roses he planted that could lift your spirits even on a rainy day.

At the top of the garden the chicken coop was another recycling project. Table scraps were mixed into the hot hash my father prepared daily for the hens. To go out in the morning and filch an egg from under a squawking hen and boil it for your breakfast is to see the immediate and delicious benefits of "waste not, want not."

In some aspects I have inherited the thrift gene.

When I take my iron kettle out of the cupboard, my husband knows soup made from homemade stock will soon be bubbling on the stove. There is never a pick left on a bone that leaves this house. Be it chicken, turkey or lamb, all the remaining skin and bones and pot "likker" are boiled up into a fragrant broth. People have laughed to see that old pot and the scraps that go into it. But they've never laughed at my soup.

No paper is ever recycled from my office unless both sides of the page have been used.

What's wrong with using a shopping bag to bring home

the groceries? They're washable, re-usable and carry a whole lot more than puny plastic bags or paper bags that rip. And they won't clog up the landfill. Before brand names paid for our television programs, we chose our own "no-name" soaps, veggies, butter and cheese and all the rest. Newspaper separated the dirty potatoes from the other items in the big leather shopping bag.

In the doctor's office the other day, I saw a familiar scene. She, a lady of Scottish extraction, had an almost empty bottle of soap in the bathroom draining into a new bottle to use up the last drop. I was impressed. If, like me, you live outside the boundaries of Scotland you may see eyebrows raised at the perfectly logical methods we use to save money, substance, and, incidentally, the environment. And why not? My husband laughs and thinks I go too far when he sees me saving a jar of jam because there is another spoonful in it. The last wee drop in the bottle is just a good as the first, be it soap or medicine or single malt whisky.

I've passed the thrift gene on to my daughter, who is an environmentalist and conservationist, and my grandson who is canny wi' his bawbees. He is only half Scottish, but has a philosophy on spending money that would make his ancestors proud. After he learns the price of something he wants, he says indignantly, "I'm not wasting my money on that!" He knows, to the penny, the amount in his bank account and has no plans to spend any of it apparently. Then, he asks, "Will you buy it for me?"

Our reputation for thrift is worldwide. We are teased about it in jokes and stories and even on the internet, where I got this gem: When the ferry company in the Western Isles charged reduced rates for vehicles transporting sheep, some customers took advantage of this and took a sheep in the back seat of their car when going to the mainland (and had the same sheep on the way back). Eventually, the company had to change the rules.

Then there's the one about the two brothers who went

into business together. At the end of the first year they tried to balance their account books, but were ten pounds short. They tried again and again, but no matter which way they tried to do it, they always came out ten pounds short. "Tell me the truth, Sandy," asked his brother, "Are you keeping a woman on the side?"

Some stories about Scottish thrift go too far:

A Scottish sergeant major went into the chemist with a damaged condom and asked, "How much to fix this and how much for a new one?"

"Sixpence to fix it; a shilling for a new one," he was told. He came back the next day and told the chemist, "The regiment says, 'Fix it.'"

By Yon Bonnie Banks

My husband, Paul the fisherman, knows that right here in Florida, despite the wonderful sunshine and ambient winter climate, there is only one thing worth getting up for on a Sunday morning ... the fishing show on television.

Aye, believe it or not folks, there are those enthusiasts who, when they can't get out on the gulf or the river or the loch themselves, will get their fix from watching grown men stand for hours on a flat boat that no sane person would risk their life on; throwing a line into the water with the same kind of focus and deliberation a surgeon would use performing a life-saving operation.

I awaken with a start, and I know it's daybreak in the swamp when I hear the television blaring and it's Dave and Hank on ESPN or OLN yelling, "Fish on."

Yes! They're all called Dave or Hank. Except when they're called Jimmy, but I won't even go there. Watching a grown man kissing a fish on the lips before I've had my coffee, I will not do.

Being a writer, I have often wondered who scripts the dialogue for these shows? Is there a market for this type of writing? Could I make any money at it?

I think I can do it. Wanna bet?

Scene 1

DAVE: *It's just a great, great day out here on beautiful Lake Whatchamacallit. Right, Hank?*
HANK: *Any day's a great day for fishing, Dave.*
(Knowing wink towards camera)
Dave rears back as line tugs.
DAVE: (Gasps) *Did you see that? Git the net.*
Dave staggers as the line breaks free.
DAVE: *Gosh darn it! Did you see the size of that fish?*
Turns away from camera to regain his composure.
DAVE: *Almost had that one in the boat.*
HANK: (Chuckles)
Yeah, Dave. That's why they call it fishin' not catchin'.

See what I mean? It's easy. But no matter how exciting the dialogue, watching other people fishing is only a little less entertaining than watching other people playing golf or meditating.

Have you ever had a conversation with an angler who is "on a bite"? I've tried swapping philosophies with a saltwater fisherman out on the Gulf of Mexico. The best I can say about the dialogue is that I advanced some deliberations in my own thought processes without interrupting his too much.

It's a perfect, sunny and calm day on St. Joseph's Sound in the Gulf of Mexico; I have had my quota of fishing for the day ... about two hours and I'm done. I am trying to comprehend the book, *Everyday Zen*, that I have brought to study.

"Hmmm. Why do you suppose Buddhists have this tradition of meditation that is so deeply embedded into their culture?" I say.

"Yeah, this hook is deeply embedded. Willya give me the pliers." He removes the hook and releases the fish.

Looking out over the Gulf, pondering family matters, the latest bad news from the Middle East, surveying Hurricane Pass, a gap between the islands, blown out by a previous storm, and wondering what the next season will bring, I return to my book and read out loud: "Zen practice isn't about a special place, or a special peace, or something other than what it is."

Ten minutes of serious philosophical ruminating later, I say, apropos of nothing, "Maybe it's because they are landlocked. Do you suppose?"

"Yeah. I think this one is deep hooked."

"Maybe it's because they had to find a substitute for fishing." Wee bit of sarcasm here, folks. I missed my lunch and it's heading toward dinnertime.

"There's a substitute for fishing?" He chokes or laughs. Enough of my musing filtered through the haze for him to assume this was the punch line of a joke.

Out on the water I take time to ponder.

Out on the pond he takes time to wander.

It's meditation. I swear it is.

No dialogue needed.

Paul fishing on Loch Lomond

But what do Scotsmen talk about when they go fishing?

I decided to take a survey. I have to admit it was not very scientific, purely anecdotal and based on the two Scottish fishermen I was able to contact before my deadline.

First, they assured me about things they DO NOT talk about, i.e. "fishing" and "blondes" and I didn't even ask about the latter.

For one thing, the names are different; they are called Robin and Jim (Jimsy to his closest associates after a nip or two).

Jimsy told me everything I ever wanted to know about fly fishing; the importance of the time of day, weather conditions, season, various stages of gnats, mosquitoes, midges; how chrysalises develop, the rippling of the wind on the water and when to switch to a Devon Lure. Jings!

Then my whole "I could write that dialogue" theory got blown out of the water; pun intended. They don't fish out of a boat or even together. No. They talk only in the car and about family or business on the way there and compare their catch on the way back.

So, here goes.

(First draft)

Scene 2

Robin and Jimsy are driving their four-by-four to Loch Lomond:

ROBIN: *And how's the wife and the bairns?*
JIMSY: *Och! They're doin' fine. Blah! Blah! Blah! And how's business?*
ROBIN: *No sae bad. Blah! Blah! Blah! Well, here we are.*

JIMSY: *OK. Do you want to go upstream first?*
ROBIN *Aye. I' ll meet ye back here in about three hours.*

(Note to camera) Cut to Robin hiking up the bank with his grandfather's creel balanced on his shoulder. He wears chest waders and a MacLean tartan scarf for good luck around his neck. Jacket w/ tartan lining (Note to costume: Matching tartans optional.) This purist has hand-tied fish lures from a secret pattern handed down through four generations. He uses hair from his Irish Setter and feathers gathered from around his bird feeder. All are displayed prominently on his moleskin cap.

There are clouds obscuring Ben Lomond.

Cut to Jimsy wearing mesh vest that barely meets over his Shetland wool sweater knitted by his mother during WWII. Leather Bushman hat is decorated like a Christmas tree with assorted lures. Size 13 green Wellies meet and match his waterproof over-trousers that are held up by braces with logo of Stirling Castle.

Carrying his lucky bamboo rod and an oversized landing net, just in case, he goes around the first bend to a chair-shaped boulder exactly the right size and sits.

Cue rain.

World travellers, John and Harriet Milne, Joyce's Mum and Dad, sent this photo to their daughter in New York, hinting it was time for a visit, c. 1960.

Mother's Day Memories

My father is cooking in the post war Scottish kitchen, back in the day when many dads did not cook. Where's Mum? He has only one dish in his repertoire ... French toast. We three kids, aged seven, four, and two, love it. No one actually bothers to ask where Mum is. She's been a bit grouchy lately anyway and doesn't want you climbing on her lap. Has anyone noticed she doesn't have a lap anymore?

There is a lot of commotion upstairs and Daddy disappears.

Right on cue Granny arrives at the back door with her big leather shopping bag.

"All right, you lot, get yourselves dressed and out to play." She dons an apron.

"But it's raining."

"Aye, that's a peety."

She doesn't care. She wants to get upstairs where Daddy and Mummy are. What is going on? Now we are curious. But whatever Granny says goes; we have to go outside. Maybe the rain will stop.

Several hours later, when the French toast is history, we clamour at the door for attention. Granny opens the door with a bundle in her arms. "This is your new wee brother."

We don't have a cabbage patch. I didn't see a stork.

Now how did that Mother's Day happen?

LUMPY PORRIDGE

In anticipation of a very important Mother's Day that turns out to be December 25, 1996, Nana and Papa travel across the United States from Florida to Oregon to arrive during an ice storm. The big event will not wait. It is the heralded first grandchild. Who decides, not only to appear on Christmas Day, but during the storm of the century in Portland, Oregon. Ice-laden trees shatter like glass; the steep hill, where the grandparents' accommodations are, is treacherous to descend and impossible to climb.

'Twas the night before Christmas … "She's ready!" We bundle the momma-to-be into the car, wide-eyed from the dawning realization that no matter what anyone said or what assurances were given or what help is being proffered, bringing another human being into the world is a shock and a surprise. Daddy-to-be gets lost on his way to the hospital. While Santa is making his rounds, Nana-to-be remembers her rusty nursing skills. Way into the night Papa brings food. Daddy reminds the patient to breathe. The protracted, painful labour is still a lonely business despite the excellent midwife. But, before that Christmas Day is over, a child is born. Christmas Day is Mother's Day that year.

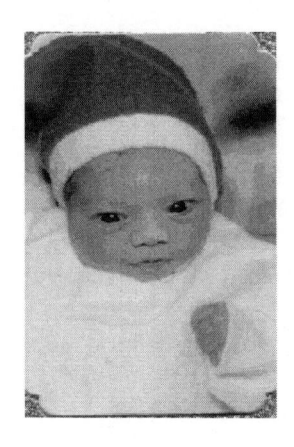

Joyce Milne D'Auria

Happy Birthday, Joshua.

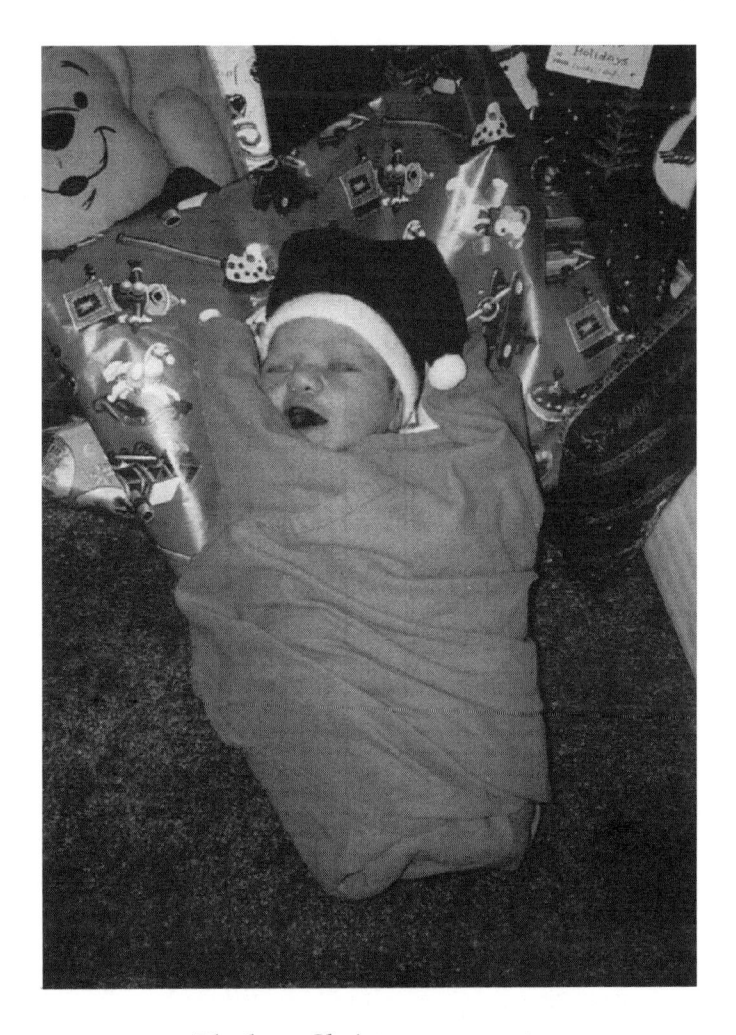

The best Christmas present ever

My good friend sits home. It's Mother's Day. Her children will call, she says, wearing a serious look of doubt. She does this every year. They never call. She feels unloved, a failure.

She calls me. It's a short call because she has to leave the line free. "I don't understand it. What did I do wrong?"

"You were/are a great Mom. They love you. The lines are probably jammed." My genuine compliments fall on deaf ears. She very successfully gave them "roots and wings." The little birds have flown. They are fulfilling the promise she always saw in them. Busy lives. Reaching for dreams. Yes, they are a bit selfish.

One call wouldn't hurt.

It's my second week as a seventeen-year-old student at the Glasgow Royal Infirmary School of Nursing, 1960. Homesickness is not in this new apprentice's independent-minded vocabulary. But it is all too hard and maybe I'll fail, and for the first time in my life I'm around strangers. All the other young women in the crisp nurses' uniforms seem so confident; many of them have had prior hospital experience. Old hands at eighteen!

The phone booth is adjacent to the nurses' lounge where the other students are chatting amiably. They are all so sophisticated, I think, and I'm a country bumpkin. While I dial, I practice excuses. "I don't feel well." "I forgot to bring my winter coat." Discarding these flimsy pretexts, I settle for the truth. "I want to come home, Mum. Please come and get me."

The phone rings ... once. The relief of my decision brings surprising tears. Twice ... sobs. Three times ... embarrassing wailing. Four, five, six. No one's home. I hang up. How could they fail me in my moment of life-changing decision?

Two apple-cheeked future nurses appear at the booth.
"You all right?"
They must have overheard my personal drama.
"Want to go out for a coffee?"

Three years later I graduate with them. We have been fast friends for years.

Mother never knew how hard it was to leave home. Perhaps I should have told her ... later. She probably would have appreciated knowing that it wasn't easy for me either. I'll mention it in my next Mother's Day card along with all the other things she'd appreciate knowing.

It's the day Mum gets breakfast in bed. In these Yoonided States Mother's Day is almost as important as Hogmanay. The chef is six years old and her cooking skills are basic but promising. The clatter in the kitchen betrays the stealth mission. A knock at the bedroom door and I give a sleepy "Who is it?"

"It's me."

"Come in. What's going on?" The door opens and a tray, perilously perched at a forty-five degree angle, makes its way towards the bed toted by a frazzled, curly-headed girl bursting with pride. "Happy Mother's Day. Surprise!"

On the menu is: boiled egg in an eggcup; toast with lots of butter and marmalade; a half saucer of tea and a half-cup of tea. My favourites.

"You did this?" I feign incredulity. It still works … not for much longer. Six is halfway to twelve. Enjoy it while it lasts, Mother.

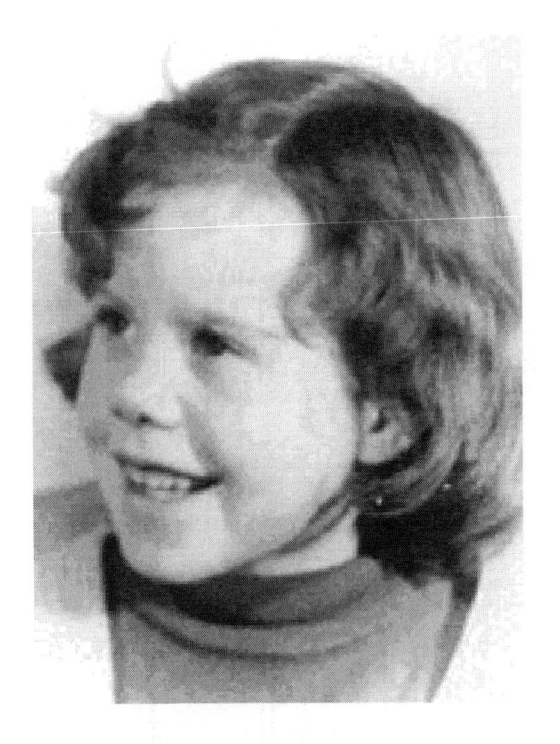

My favourite chef
Linda MacIntyre Frame

My old Mum takes the flight from Glasgow. She's been a world traveller all her life. John, my father, was her constant companion, but she's widowed now. I meet her in Tampa, Florida. She has shrunk. Without her mate to cook for, she forgets to eat. She has forgotten to take her medicine too. Her blood pressure is off the charts. I am afraid to leave her alone.

On her second day she passes out and I rush her to the clinic. I am afraid to leave her alone. Nervous and scared, I supervise her medicines; enforce her low salt diet (she doesn't eat); leave a "sitter" when I have to be at work.

She is serene. She and the sitter have great wee blethers. She sits by the window and watches the tides and the shore birds. After about two weeks of the planned one month visit she says, "I think I'll go home now."

I worry. Was it something I said? Is she afraid of being admitted to an American hospital and using her savings? Have I spent enough time with her? But the questions go unasked, as is the case so oft en between mother and daughter.

The parting at the airport is our final farewell. She says so and I, of course, disagree. She is right.

Her new son-in-law quietly observes my meltdown ... they are very much alike. Funny how we choose our mates.

"What happened?" I wail.

"She came to make sure you were all right, then she went home," he says, confident he passed the mother-in-law test.

LUMPY PORRIDGE

Scottish Grandma gets to meet her American grandchild for the first time in New York Joyce, Harriet, and Linda.

Old Friends are the Best

Don't you love to connect with old, I mean REALLY old, friends?

Before I name any names I have to inject a disclaimer here. These friends are old only in respect to the number of years we have popped in and out of each other's lives.

Don't you love the easy way you can pick up the pieces after twenty years? They look different at first, as though you are seeing them through a veil. The years have changed both of you. But that is superficial. Their essence is the same as you remembered

After a few hours or even minutes together, the same youthful exuberance emerges in your sharing. You both start to sound like you did twenty years ago, maybe even thirty or forty. No! It's not possible, not forty! You revert to story telling in a dialogue of accents and even codes. They make you laugh at things no one else would appreciate (especially not your grown children; who are often affronted at such displays of senile adolescence.)

And the jokes.

About the jokes ... well never mind. You had to be there.

Our group that goes back to the Glasgow Royal Infirmary School of Nursing 1960 is scattered across the globe. In our final year of training, six of us shared an apartment on Queen Margaret Drive in Glasgow. I understand that is now very upscale real estate. At the time it was a place for six very hard working lassies to rest up between the nine or twelve hour shifts.

Or sometimes a place to get on your party duds and go out on the town.

Or sometimes a place to throw a shindig.

*Mhairi, Joyce, and Anne, all decked out for
New Year's Eve. 1962*

And party we did. We must have had the best neighbours in Glasgow or they were totally deaf.

"Remember the party when a whole bunch of sailors showed up uninvited and drunk and overly boisterous and Meg literally threw them out?"

It was a bit scary because we were on the fifth floor and the railing was only a few feet from the door where they were so rudely ejected. But since there were no navy blue clad bodies on the ground floor in the morning she had obviously made the right decision.

Meg (and Jim) and I laughed about this event when we met up in Toowoomba in 1979. I visited my brother Robert in Brisbane, Australia, and since I was "in the neighbourhood" I dropped in.

Anne and Mhairi (and Robin and Colin) came to see me in New York, where I lived, on the St. Lawrence River, for Ne'erday c. 1965, and I have the photos with the high heels, coiffed hair, and ultra-slender figures in sleek sheaths to prove it. And I have "dropped in" on them from Quebec to Toronto to Vancouver as they "flitted" to different Canadian cities over the intervening years.

Beryl, the only one who remained in Scotland, made the rounds here in North America in 1995. Before taking off for Vancouver, via Sedona, she stayed with us in Florida. We went to Cypress Gardens and had afternoon tea there and visited the butterfly garden (a favourite of mine) and hummed along with the Elvis impersonator. It is an American theme park, after all.

On our boat we went to Dunedin out to the beautiful beach on Caladesi Island. But her most memorable day was the morning she observed my husband, Paul, managing to wreck the davit his boat hung on and tumble after it into the bayou. Her only regret was that her camera was upstairs.

Beryl has been my travelling companion on trips to Scotland and France. Her indefatigable energy carried us from Biarritz to her place in the medieval village of Salies-de-Béarn in 2005.

It was like a sixteenth century movie set. We got there on the long French weekend and the place was deserted. Suddenly, as though the troupe had been sent from central casting, the village square filled with people carrying their morning newspapers and the ubiquitous baguette, walking their dogs, and greeting us with "Bonjour, Madame."

In Salies I lost the stone out of my diamond ring in the swimming pool. I discovered it missing when I was in the shower and let out a blood-curdling scream. Beryl likened it to the scene from "Psycho" (funny one).

We explored Scotland like tourists, starting out from her

home, with its signature grand piano in the kitchen, on the Moray Firth and on to Rannoch and Dundee where I collected information for books in progress. Spontaneous tourists that we are, we found such treasures as a Zen garden near Banff with a tearoom that served the best Cullen Skink (creamy fish soup, for the uninitiated). On a rainy day in Rannoch Moor we filled the empty church with our dulcet tones in a duet from the songbook.

And last year on a trip to Portland, Oregon "since I was in the neighbourhood" I dropped in on Mhairi (and Colin) in their beautiful mountainside home in West Vancouver for a few days. Within hours her Highland and my (slightly) North American accent were becoming more and more Glesca', with a little help from our friend Colin, as the tall tales were told.

Tip to travellers: "Don't eat the pepperoni from the Granville Market in Vancouver no matter how much Mhairi praises it."

"Just take a wee bite. It's delicious."

"No Mhairi. I never eat that."

"But you have to try it."

"Snap went my front tooth at the gum."

I had to go out on the elegant evening they planned to the opera: gap-toothed.

Old friends are the best but they can lead you astray.

Astray!

What a great idea!

How about a reunion? I was thinking of Las Vegas.

*Joyce, Mhairi, and Beryl.
Old friends reunite in Scotland 2006*

The Blonde

My Husband and the Blonde

I admit I don't like cars, vehicles, automobiles, hot rods, wee jalopies, Cadillacs, Fords, Beemers etc. I tolerate them for transportation purposes only. And I especially don't like lorries, trucks or great big, noisy, petrol/gas-guzzling sixteen wheeler behemoths used primarily to intimidate me on the highway. Sorry, lads.

Now, I know this will seem like a strange aversion to some, and it is definitely not inherited. My father always had a car, even in Scotland soon after the war, when that was something of a rarity. His car was his pride and joy. Back in the day we took family trips in the Morris Minor and later in the Austin Eight, but the roads were not crammed. The novelty value overrode everything back then, even the carsickness from the fumes (which Dad denied existed.) Going for a wee drive was a special jaunt and Sunday outings were a thrill. As we flew along at 30 an hour the scenery was a blur. We never knew what adventures we would run into.

We kids never tired of one particular escapade: The Electric Brae.

In Largs, on our way to Croy Shore, we stopped the car, put it in neutral, and seem to glide up the Electric Brae. Why? The slope of 1 in 86 upwards from Craigencroy Glen creates an optical illusion so a stationary car appears to roll uphill. At least that's what Dad said, but we kids knew it was magic.

The destination wasn't always important. Getting there was the thing.

Finally we got to Loch Lomond or Loch Ness or Largs or some other exotic destination where they had an ice-cream stand and the opportunity to paddle in some frigid water.

Ok. I admit to some good times on car rides.

The view over the Firth of Clyde looking towards Ailsa Craig and the Mull of Kintyre is spectacular, as long as the rain stays away.

Sunday excursion also offered the rare opportunity to be part of "adult" conversations.

"Wis that the road to Loch Lomond ye just made me miss? Och, I'll have to turn back at the next farm road." Note the insinuation that his getting lost was our fault!

"We have to stop and get fresh eggs, anyway. And look there's a place that has gooseberries, too."

"Och, we cannae stop now. There's too much traffic." Which was rarely true, unless you count a car stopped by the side of the road with a flat, a farm tractor moving at five miles an hour, and a collie taking a nap in the sun in the middle of the road. Unscheduled stops were not welcomed. My father had a destination. He drove; Mum viewed the scenery and doled out caramels.

In the days before fast foods, the stop signals came from Mum too. "Let's have a cuppa." When the driver was finally outvoted, the car came to a screeching halt. The boot was opened and the primus started up, and soon the salmon sandwiches with the obligatory thin pink line in the middle of the pan bread (more butter than salmon) appeared. We prayed it wouldn't rain on our picnic, but possibly since we'd missed church for this spree, our prayers often went unanswered.

My distaste for cars is probably related to the sheer number of them now. In earlier times in the spaces in front of houses children would skip rope, play football, cricket, bounce balls off stone walls, and perform derring-do with a gird and cleat down the middle of the road. Now they are warned within an inch of their lives. "Stay off the road."

But male members of my family have a love affair with cars. Dad finished up with a big black Daimler as a universal remedy for his midlife crisis.

My cousin I stay with in Balfron, Scotland, owned, as of last month, gathering dust in his garage, a vintage Jaguar, an MGTD, a Morris Minor (and if he doesn't cut down on the pie 'n chips he's going to need a Morris Major!). Of course he doesn't drive any of those; he gets to work in a station wagon.

My husband is off the charts with his car collection here in Florida. Our garage looks like a scene from a Glasgow motor show. He has, as of yesterday, four classic British cars including a 1969 MGC with straight 6, (not sure what that means, but guys are impressed.) This one draws admiring glances from both sexes. It took eighteen months from delivery on the flat bed truck to the final coat of primrose paint. My daughter aptly dubbed it "The Blonde" for its impact on our marital bliss.

Do you see a pattern here? He likes OLD BRITISH things. *Which is lucky for me, being an old British person.*

Also in the fleet is a 1969 MGB GT, which did *not* need a paint job as it is a gorgeous shade of "Jewel Green" but "needed" upgrading from a 4-cylinder to a V8. It is now officially a MGB GT V8 Sebring featuring a Rover 3.5. Whatever that means.

AND THERE'S MORE, as the adverts say:

A Cavalry blue 1981 TR 8 Roadster is used on weekends, and, in the works is a disassembled 1973 MGB V8 Sebring with the Rover 3.9, color yet to be determined.

Och! It makes ma heid hurt!

Riding farther than ten miles from the garage requires the addition of a toolbox in the boot ... or a walk home. (I exaggerate.) But this I do know, these beauties do not arrive in purring, pretty perfection; they need work. Lots of it. These vehicles are not for show and not really for transportation. Their purpose is to be fixed, painted, kept running, upgraded and taken for short drives to test them ... and to be polished.

OK, I admit, I don't get it.

Paul has to actually like a person before he will sell one of these beauties. He has only met one person so far he liked well enough to let one go. That was the one I backed into in the driveway (but that's another story ... a sadder tale.)

But I just got a car that might change my mind about vehicular travel. It's excellent transportation, shiny silver with grey upholstery; it runs silently most of the time and gets 50+ mpg, answers your telephone, knows when to shift gears, tells you where to go (politely), and the seats adjust perfectly to accommodate a five foot woman. The five CD player will be great on a long trips and the air is thermostatically controlled. And all this with the touch of a button.

I just got a Prius.

I think there is a button for making coffee too, but I haven't found it yet.

Guess I'll have to read the manual.

The Blonde and the Redhead

The Scottish Grannies

The author flanked on both sides by
hundred plus years of love and
hard-earned wisdom

A Childhood in Lanarkshire

Kisses on the Bottom

"Och! Give her a wee sweety." He took the poke of Dolly Mixtures from Granny's hesitant grasp.

My Uncle George would give me anything, especially if it wasn't good for me.

"She'll no be able tae eat her dinner, ye daft wee tattiebogle." Granny's pleas were half-hearted.

"Watch out, auld yin." He made as if to grab her. His warning made her squeal but not from fright. He was the world's worst tickler and nobody, but nobody, was safe from his attacks — not even his mother.

"Give me a hand here." She inclined her head towards the kitchen where she'd spent most of the morning. "Yer sisters will be home from the Buttercup in ten minutes and the table's no set. They'll come in here chitterin'. It's cold in that dairy. Break up the smoored dross on that fire and brighten the place up a bit."

She looked at her son, shook her head, and sighed. "They're no expectin' tae see you in that uniform. They're goin' tae have conniptions."

He winked, flashed his broadest grin and sealed our alliance by sneaking me the forbidden "sweety", which I sucked noisily.

"Wheesht, wean. Ye'll get yer uncle in a spot o' bother."

I giggled and shrugged.

From the second floor kitchen window of the tenement, Granny was able to see anyone emerging from the close. "Here's Nan. Nettie can't be far behind. Make yerself useful get these tatties and neeps mashed, the mince is ready."

George ignored her. He'd always enjoyed cooking before but probably thought that a soldier in the British army was not supposed to do "women's work." He was concentrating on the fire, jabbing the poker between the grids. Soon, he had a blaze roaring gloriously in the grate.

I hopped off the chair and ran to the door. He gently grasped my arm as I ran past him. "Wait, come back here. Don't tell them I'm here."

He pressed his index finger to his lips and hid behind the door. Then, suddenly remembering, he dashed out to retrieve his khaki duffel bag and hide it behind him. The camouflage worked well here in the living room with its beige wallpaper, toned down with a year's worth of soot—brown uniform, brown hair, brown bag, brown door.

I had been waiting for this moment. Now I could give her the letter. It was my job to give my aunts the treasured letters from their husbands far, far away fighting in the war. She'd be so happy.

The best part for me was the return letters that my aunts wrote to their sweethearts. I got to put the kisses on the bottom, with help, of course. I can't write properly yet; someone needs to help me hold the pen. I stuffed the envelope under my jersey. It would be a surprise.

Nan burst into the room, rosy-cheeked from the bitter March wind, energised from her long walk and excited about the prospect of news from Uncle Hugh.

She gave me a quick hug and kiss, took a minute to warm herself at the crackling fire, and called to Granny. "Has the postman been here yet, Maw?"

But before I could astonish her with the envelope with all the colourful stamps on it, she let out a scream that scared me and brought Granny running from the kitchen with the potato masher in her hand.

"Who's here?" Nan asked her, eyes glued to the military cap on the table; her face had gone pale.

"It's not him, Nan. He's still overseas. Your daft brother jyned up."

Right on cue, her brother pushed the door back and revealed himself in his glorious khaki uniform with the British army insignia, and gave her a cheeky salute.

Och! I couldn't believe it. She started to cry then and say things that didn't make any sense. "I thought it was my man. Why did you? Oh! George, how could ye do it? I thought you were deferred. Another one tryin' tae get killed." She ran to the only other room of the tenement crying like a baby.

"Sit up and eat your dinner." My grandmother ordered, picking me up and plonking me on a chair with two cushions. "And try not to get it all over ye."

Now everybody was in a bad mood. I carefully pushed the mince aside (it had onions in it), identified and removed pieces of turnip that had migrated to the mashed potatoes, and began stuffing the creamy spuds into my mouth. Granny had put butter and milk on them. I was about to savour the last spoonful, when my aunt appeared from the front room. She'd stopped crying—barely. Her face was white; some of the face powder had spilled on to her blue wool twin set, but her eyes were still red.

She came over to where I sat. "Sorry, ma wee pet, it wasn't your fault."

I smiled at her and spooned the last mouthful of potatoes down; glad she was happy again. Then they did a lot of adult talk about the war and the rationing and the blackout—the usual stuff, while I pushed the mince to a corner of the plate trying to make the mound of offensive food seem smaller so Granny would believe I'd eaten some of it. (It never worked.)

When my other auntie got home she had a screaming fit too about her wee brother going off to die in some foreign country. I almost forgot the letter in all the uproar, until I patted my full tummy and my jumper made a crinkly sound.

"Look what I gots!"

I whipped it out from under my jersey. Surely this would turn the tide of ill temper.

Nettie took it; inspected the envelope; her face fell. "It's for you," she said and threw it at her sister. Now it was her turn to run ben the house crying.

Aunt Nan read the letter while we watched her going from a frown to a blush, to a wide smile that lit up her pretty face. "He says he'll have two weeks leave in July. He'll be home soon." She crushed the letter to her breast. "I'm going to answer it right away."

I sat in Granny's chair waiting patiently for my aunt to finish. It took forever; she'd look up at the ceiling, smile, then write a little more.

"You'd better finish that letter and get back to work before you get the sack," Granny warned.

Aunt Nan scribbled the last few lines quickly.

"Did ye leave some room on the page?" I asked. "Can I? Can I? Can I, please? Can I put the kisses on the bottom?"

"Of course. Come over here."

I climbed onto her lap. She'd left a big blank space on the page for me to put my own personal message to my uncle.

XXXXXXXXXXXXXXXXX

Joyce

Nan and Hugh Shimmins c.1943
He is finally on leave and she has a
blue velvet dress for the occasion.

*The Waverley just dropped off the Milne clan
in Rothesay c.1950*

The Glesca' Fair

Once upon a time in Scotland, when the Canary Islands were not even considered as a holiday destination for people on our street; when the south of Spain was exotic; when we didn't even know where Dubai was (or Dubya, for that matter), when the Disney name meant Mickey Mouse cartoons, not a place to spend your vacation, and cruises were for the very wealthy — we went to that famous resort on the isle of Bute, Rothesay, for two weeks in July ... the second fortnight. Everybody did.

It was the Glasgow Fair, a deep-rooted institution going back, they say, to the Middle Ages when there was an actual fair on the Glasgow Green with menageries, freak shows, tumblers, waxworks, whisky drinking and who knows what kind of medieval shenanigans.

Otherwise referred to as the Glesca' Ferr, which is not really a fair anymore but a time-honoured tradition whereby people, not just in Glasgow but all over Lanarkshire, drop everything they are doing in the middle of July, take their holidays, and head "Doon the Watter" meaning down the Clyde River (for the uninitiated). No foreign bazaars or fragrant spices or belly dancers or even sunshine, just two weeks in Scotland's favourite familiar holiday destination off the west coast of Scotland.

Och, it was rerr! Two weeks of bliss interrupted by the

occasional downpour on the Thursday, followed by a whole day of rain on Friday, followed by sunny showers on the weekend, and maybe some clearin' on Monday.

Preparations began at least a month prior to the "Fair." First we packed. A wicker hamper appeared and remained in the sitting room (the room verboten to us kids) until the huge receptacle with the rope handles groaned with every piece of decent clothing we owned, cleaned and pressed.

For the first two weeks in July we kids looked like ragamuffins in the duds not deemed good enough to take on holiday. The amount of perishable food in the larder was reduced to scraps, in preparation for closing the house for two weeks. Jelly pieces on plain breid for tea.

The anticipation; the excitement; the sleepless nights. The upheaval was worth it. The journey started with a train ride, or a drive down the Clydeside if you were lucky enough to have a car. We had a Morris Eight. Three adults (at least one granny accompanied us), four weans, and a hamper crammed into a wee car that got from Coatbridge to Wemyss Bay on a cuppa petrol.

Once there, we poured onto the immense wooden dock into a crush of nervous parents herding excited weans. I desperately tried to keep track of my parents and wee brothers in the melee, till we reached the precarious-looking gangplank that seemed unlikely to support the number of eager passengers climbing aboard the *Waverly* or the *Jeanie Deans* for the trip to the island.

The horn blasted, the engines roared and set the giant paddles rumbling into motion, and we were off. My wild brothers perched precariously on the guardrails, where they had climbed in order to wave hankies at absolute strangers there on the dock as if we were heading out on a long trans-Atlantic journey instead of the few miles from Wemyss Bay to Rothesay.

The sea air refreshed us after breathing the city air laced with factory and coal fire smoke for eleven months. The sight of verdant hills arcing down to windswept shores is still my favourite scene. Nowhere else in the world do gulls scream with a Scottish accent!

We disembarked at the pier in Rothesay and drove a mile or so on the coast road to Craigmore, where we descended on the poor boarding-house owner, who must have cringed to see this ravenous horde flooding in year after year. Despite the ice cream, the Edinburgh Rock and the candy floss we devoured on our daily trips to the beach or the castle, we could still return to Mrs. Magill's and consume three square meals a day.

My memories of our traditional two-week holiday in Rothesay go back to when I was barely three. I lost my mother on the promenade. I was just lollygagging along in my own little world when, Oops! There she was — gone. Undeterred, I walked to the first familiar looking door and presented myself with my curly-headed credentials and some casual concern about Mum's disappearance.

"Och, it's the wee Milne lassie frae Coatbrig'. Ur ye lost, Hen?"

"No, my mum is."

Who they were or how they knew me I can't recall, but in no time my father was summoned, and he arrived, relieved I am sure, and rode me back to our hotel on his shoulders, an extra bonus adventure.

There were always exciting tales to bring home and share when we returned to school. One year I returned proudly wearing a shiny white cast.

I was about age eight, walking on the promenade, when I got in a tussle with John, my oldest brother, about the ownership of a shell collection, and took a spill on the hard pavement. (I was pushed.) After a couple of days someone got the idea that maybe my left arm needed some medical care. In the tiny island hospital I was x-rayed and had the novel experience of coming out of a chloroform fog. I was the centre of attention for a while with the shiny white cast on my "green-stick" fractured wrist.

Remember the Punch and Judy shows? We sat on the wooden benches anticipating the curtain opening on the show. We cheered and booed. That poor puppet took so many blows to the head for our entertainment.

Then came the talent show for us kiddies. I waited nervously for the opportunity to perform. "Who's next?"

I jumped up. I'd been practicing my Carmen Miranda impersonation for months. "Oh. I, I, I, I, I, I like you very much. I, I, I, I, I, I, think you're grand …" Where were the Hollywood talent scouts?

And the "Winter Gardens!" The local music hall featured singers talented and awful, skits we found hilarious, and jokes we could retell on our return to Coatbridge. We went twice a week, each time they changed the show. The goofy sketches and spoofs made us howl, and by the time we came home we knew by heart all the popular songs of the day.

We have whole albums of Rothesay photos snapped by the entrepreneur who photographed everybody going by on the esplanade. There's Granny with a hat on. Let's not get too casual! There's one with my three brothers playing miniature golf.

How about those fishing expeditions? For a couple of bob you bought a frame with a length of green string wound on it and a hook on the end designed to catch crabs … maybe. Many patient hours later after hanging over the sea wall eagerly anticipating a tug on your drop line you might have a few squirming crustaceans in your sand bucket.

Tell me, why do children not feel the cold like other beings? The sight of a sandy beach, the waves lapping and the knowledge that there is a brand new bathing suit at the bottom of the hamper makes it irrelevant that the temperature is barely in the sixties. Even then there was always some idiot splashing around, waving their mottled arms, and yelling, "It's OK once you're in." Never trust anyone who says that.

Remember "chittery bites?" That's what we called the sweetie, my mum's favourite, Cadbury's chocolate that was placed in your mouth to stop your teeth from chattering after you emerged from the frigid water of Ettrick Bay. And who can forget sand castles labouriously built and the countless hours spent running back and forth from the ocean with a bucket of water in an endless endeavour to fill the moat. And checking the next day to see if your castle survived the tide. Of course, it never did.

Every Glesca' Fair had its own unique memories and the years you came back sporting a tan ... you felt like a film star.

*Wee brothers John and Robert
and friend Ian.*

Scottish Wurrds

BLETHER: talk foolishly or too much (about nothing or something untrue).

"Ah was goin' down the street for ma messages when yon Mrs. Hardie came out her close. Ah think she times it. Couldn't get away from her bletherin' aboot the meenister at the Wee Free, and how her man came home from the pub without his wallies and he can't get another set of teeth on the National Health this year, and about the price of mince. Jings! Had tae rush hame tae put the soup on."

IT'S A PEETY: This is an appropriate response for just about anything (even blethers).

"The Rangers Celtic game on Saturday wis rained oot."
"Aye, it's a peety."

"Ah got a skelf in ma finger, yesterday."
"Aye, that's a peety."

It can be noncommittal:

"Ma husband lost his wallies at the Big Tree Bar."
"Aye, tha's a peety."

"Ma wife's been girnin' tae go tae the pictures."
"Aye, that's a peety."

"We're goin' tae Rothesay this year."
"Aye, that's a peety.

Going for the Messages

Now people get everything in a supermarket, but I remember when "going for your messages" entailed a long walk up the street carrying an oversized leather shopping bag. For many women it was a daily event. Only so much could be carried in one trip. In those days few women worked. Unless you consider doing laundry by hand and hanging it out on the line, preparing a three-course dinner midday, beating carpets, and washing windows once a week as work, and, of course "going for your messages" or going shopping, as they say elsewhere. We Scots were carefully taught how to conserve, how to stretch a pound or a dollar.

At a very early age I was assigned the shopping mission on a Saturday morning. My mother worked and kept house. This important task took some planning. I listened to the usual instructions. "Here's the list and the money and if there's any change ye can get some sweeties ... and come straight home."

So there is the mission, the funding, the reward, and the goal. With ten shillings wrapped in a note from my mum that details my intended purchases, I set out down Blair Road along King Street to Bank Street.

First, drop off two pairs of school shoes at the cobbler to be re-soled (for the second time). Imagine the mileage on those stiff leather shoes. "And two pairs of black laces and one pair of brown, please."

Next, on to the fruiterer and into the bottom of the bag goes a 'halfastane' of new tatties covered with last week's *Coatbridge and Airdrie Advertiser*. On top a few apples, a turnip, half a head of cabbage, and two pounds of onions. Mmmm, sounds like soup to me.

Next, hurry along to the Buttercup, a dairy store, where my aunt is working today. "Mum says I'm to pick up four quarter pounds of butter."

She knows exactly what is required to set an elegant tea table and has it ready. She carefully wraps four little squares of butter with a raised thistle pattern on each. "Oh, and I'll need …" I consult my note and Aunt Nan respectfully waits on me like any other customer, "… half a pound of Cheshire."

At the baker I pick up a pan loaf and half a dozen tea bread.

The bag is getting heavier and I still have to go to the florists. "If you have any money left for a wee booky o' flowers." For one and sixpence I get enough to decorate the sideboard and the dining table.

Mission accomplished, I trot proudly back across King Street and up Blair Road.

In my absence Mum, on her day off from work, has the house in tiptop shape for the weekend, and after the flowers are arranged in two vases, the food is deposited in the pantry.

The proud wee butter patties sit on a marble shelf awaiting their presentation on the Sunday tea table.

Halfway around the world and decades later, I still take my shopping bags to the supermarket, and I get some strange looks. Sometimes the checkout person has tried to charge me for them. Aye, right!

Now in 2015 more people take their cloth bags to the supermarket. But back then I got some compliments. I'm a trendsetter. Can't help myself.

I heard such things as, "What a good idea."

"If everyone did this there would be a lot less waste."

"You can put a lot in these things."

I didn't always conserve in this way. At first when I came to these Yoonided States I participated vigorously in the "disposable" society: "Throw it away; get a new one." The excessive packaging, the double bagging, the pre-prepared foodless food, all seemed like symbols of modernity and affluence and, of course, it would never end. But wait. We are learning that my (our) waste of resources has consequences.

I wonder what my carbon footprint was in Scotland in 1958 compared to what it is in the USA now.

We Scots have been known—in fact, we've been famous—for our thrift. A few jokes told at our expense, come to mind. Well, with the population using up precious forest at an alarming rate, and creating out of control pollution, was there ever a better time to set an example?

Was there ever a more appropriate and noble cause than conserving our resources? So, maybe you are considering cutting down on fuel, buying a more efficient car perhaps, or changing your lightbulbs to the CFL type. Here's something else you can do.

Remember, all those pesky plastic bags are petroleum-based. Throw a few string and canvas bags in the back of your car the next time you go down the street for your messages; walk if you can, and remember to get a note from yer mither and buy a wee booky of flowers if ye've any money left.

LUMPY PORRIDGE

*How to make a plate of lumpy porridge
more interesting*

*This was my best attempt at map-making with a plate of porridge.
Don't laugh; it wasn't easy.*

Take Yer Lumps

We weren't morning people at my house in Coatbridge back in the day. More crabbit than chipper before we had our morning cuppa and warmed our rear ends at the kitchen stove.

Our cheerful, busy Mum was the only exception. "Eat yer porridge. It's good for ye."

Oh, no, the dreaded lumpy breakfast. We kids preferred toast with cheese or marmalade. We begged for Kellogg's cornflakes or better yet one of Mum's big breakfasts.

"Oh, no! Not porridge again." We four children whispered round the table. We'd have said it out loud, but back then complaining about the haute cuisine got you nowhere but left sitting at the kitchen table until your plate was clean or someone came along and removed your skeleton.

Well, that's a slight exaggeration but knowwhitahmean?

My mother's porridge, God rest her soul, was not her crowning achievement. Lumps! Yes, I'm sorry to say. Big lumps!

Now I have to rush to her defence. She made the best Ham 'n Eggs in Lanarkshire and I have friends and family who will attest to this. Could she wield an iron frying pan. She'd light the gas cooker with a match, and almost before its violet flame could cheer you, your hungry heart leapt with joy as the lard hit the pan with a satisfying sizzle. From the pantry appeared an overflowing plate of Ayrshire bacon, black pudding, and at least two shapes of sausages—links and sliced. While this mélange was filling the kitchen with an aroma that cannot be adequately described, eggs filched from under our own squawking hens, and potato scones were lined up ready to be added at the moment when enough of the flavoured fat had been rendered in the frying pan. A nice homegrown tomato from my father's greenhouse would garnish the dish in season.

At the table a pot of fresh tea, some of Aunt Nan's homemade marmalade, good butter, and a heaping plate of plain bread toasted. Awright!

But porridge, I'm sorry. It was a disaster.

On a recent trip to Scotland, my husband partook generously at each Bed and Breakfast of the big breakfast AND the porridge. This is not recommended. Take one or t'other. Not both. Though he is not Scottish he believes in getting what he paid for even if he has to suffer for it. Suffer he did.

But a diet of the delicious fatty food aforementioned leads to some wee problems. I and my cousins are at an age when we compare cholesterol scores.

Cousin Gordon, from Coatbridge, recently whispered to me his cholesterol level, adding, "The doctor says it's no' bad *'for the region'*."

Oops! "For the region." What does that mean? Sounds ominous.

Yes, the diet of my youth cannot be the diet of my advancing years. Unfortunately, my regional cholesterol score has carried over into the New World.

Which takes us back to porridge.

Robert Burns called parritch, "Chief of Scotia's Food." Do you suppose he knew that: "While some people frown at the idea of sugar on porridge, others not only approve but suggest a tot of whisky. Each to their own!" This online from the *Rampant Scotland* site.

Traditionally, Scots put salt on their porridge. We grew

up adding sugar. Probably an English tradition we got from our maternal grandmother from Burnley, England.

And while I was online I found a recipe for my aunt's oatmeal stuffing. A bonus!

You have no idea the amount of information that is online about porridge; I don't think Rabbie Burns knew that:

Porridge has more protein than other cereals; keeps your blood sugar even; is easy on the stomach; reduces your risk of heart disease; increases serotonin (the feel good brain chemical), and reduces your regional cholesterol.

OK, Mum. I'll eat it.

And I do. No Lipitor for me.

Armed with my spurtle, the obligatory wee stick for stirring the porridge, and a bag of steel-cut Scottish oats, I drag my crabbit self into the kitchen and boil water in my non-stick pot and gradually add the oats and stir.

Forgot to tell you, Mum, Granny showed me how to cook parritch … without lumps.

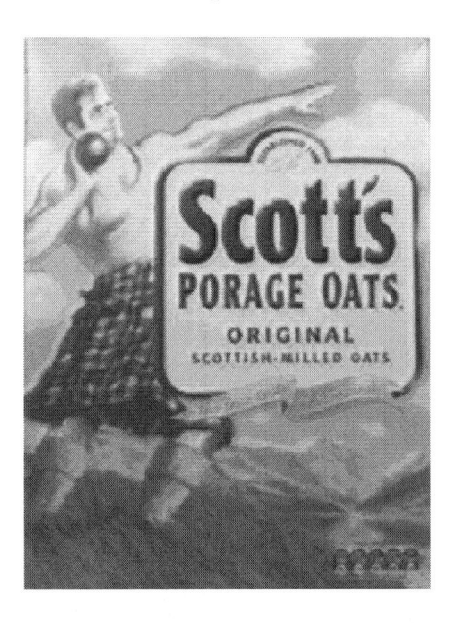

And Even More Scottish Wurrds

GIRN: complain, whine, grumble, snarl, grimace (it usually does not produce tears and is often halted for periods of time when the girner is distracted).

GREETIN': Crying, lamenting, complaining, grumbling (much wetter than girnin').

A wean girnin' and greetin' a' day will surely make yer heid sair.

My mother applied Cadbury's Hazelnut Chocolate as necessary to her offspring's wee eager mouths for either condition.

Thruppence Worth, Please

My love for fish began at an early age. The fishmonger's shop was next to our hardware store in the village of Baillieston, Lanarkshire. "I'll run next door and get a finnan haddie (smoked haddock) for our dinner." When we heard our mother saying that, we were in for a treat.

I've travelled round the world and had occasion to compare many other types and varieties of fish dishes.

Shrimp on the barbee in a coastal town near Brisbane, Australia, was one of my most memorable moments on my visit to my brother Robert, who lives there. He called them prawns. The name "shrimp" is inadequate to describe these large delicious crustaceans. Down Under they seem to wash everything down with beer, except perhaps the creamy cake called Pavlova, a melt-in-your-mouth treat; with that they serve tea.

Some years later, I ate sushi, for the first time, in Campbell River on Vancouver Island and offered polite compliments to the smiling Asian chef. But just between you an' me an' the gatepost—it tasted awfy like raw fish. But the wine was excellent.

My earliest experience with raw seafood was at the famed Oyster Bar in New York City my very first day in these Yoonided States. Got that experience out of the way!

I've eaten bass, cooked in bacon fat, on a chilly morning on the shores of Lake Ontario. Mmmm! My own catch. Lots of hot coffee was the beverage of choice.

As you can tell by now, I am quite the expert on seafood cuisine, so take my word on this. A visit to New Orleans would not be complete without lunch at Antoine's. Order Shrimp Gumbo with crusty French bread, wash it down with a glass of Chablis. For dinner I recommend Pompano en Papillote, which, to the uninitiated, is fish cooked in parchment paper.

Which brings me to my point: Fish wrapped in paper is not exclusive to French cuisine. It's been a favourite of many Scots, myself included, for years.

What is a fish supper but "Haddie en Papillote?"

Unforgettable dining experiences, in Scotland, started for me at an early age. I've told you my Mum took great pains to give us a Guid Christian upbringing. It included midweek holiness meetings, which may not sound too exciting, BUT we had to pass the fish 'n chip shop on the way home. We kids started begging for a poke of chips almost before we'd cleared the church steps and became more insistent as we approached the Night Star chip shop, our own wee corner of heaven.

Whinin' and girnin' worked as well back then as they do for kids today. "Please, Mum, please, can ah jist have thruppence worth?"

"No! Ye had yer tea."

More begging; maybe even some greetin'. "I'll share a poke wi' Wee Robert."

"I'm switherin'." That meant she might change her mind. Since by now we'd turned the corner onto Whifflet Street and were near our goal, her ambivalence was a good sign. Or was it?

Now the divine, tantalizing aroma of deep vats of bubbling fat assailed our nostrils and filled the cold night air with overwhelming enticement. We knew our mother was not immune to the temptation. She would generally give in under pressure with a, "Well, all right, this time. But wait till ye get home tae eat them. Or ye'll get grease all over yer good clothes."

It was a compromise we could live with. She'd buy a couple of fish suppers and four bags of chips, one each for her four weans.

Later on, when I was older, maybe ten or so, I would be sent off to the midweek meeting all by myself. I had a little racket going on at that time: the acceptable amount for the collection plate was sixpence. I got exactly that, wrapped in a piece of newspaper to be opened quietly before the offering. Hand in pocket, I'd feel the wrapped money as I left the house and could immediately tell if it was a small silver sixpence or two thrupenny pieces.

Yes, you've guessed it, one thrupenny piece went to my guilty pleasure and the other went into the collection plate to expiate my sins.

"Thruppence worth, please."

The big greasy poke filled with chips was set, at eye level, just within my reach on the high stainless steel counter. I stretched up to take the culinary delight in my left hand, leaving my right hand free to grasp the oversized shaker, and apply a generous amount of salt to the long, golden, shiny fingers of potato. Next came the malted vinegar. It was impossible to get enough of the aromatic stuff on the chips without creating a rivulet down my arm, soaking the sleeve of my Fair-Isle jersey. The smell would be a dead giveaway when I got home. Too late to worry.

Upstairs on the bus, I made short work of the feast, ignoring the envious glances and the twitching noses of fellow passengers, then wiped my hands on my school blazer.

When I was about fifteen, and getting ten shillings a week pocket money, I graduated to buying my own fish suppers, after a night at the pictures, which was usually a double feature, a black and white British film, then, a favourite of mine, Doris Day with her three-foot-wide smile dancing through life without a care.

Then out into the rain with one thought in mind. A fish supper! Fish caught in Aberdeen, delivered that morning, slapped around in a batter before your eager eyes, and fried in seconds to a sweet tenderness, surrounded by a crispy coating, topped up with a generous portion of my favourite gourmet potato treat. A feast for a princess, or an aspiring Hollywood actress.

Wash it all down with a bottle of Irn-bru.

Talk aboot yer memorable moments!

The Joy-ce of Cooking

It doesn't take much to turn my mind towards food or eating or cooking. I have to think about it every day because, as a family, we rarely eat out; everything gets cooked from scratch ... it's a full-time job. Fortunately, I like to cook as well as eat. It is part of my creativity. And my creativity, I have come to understand, evolves out of chaos. You should see my kitchen after the Sunday dinner goes in the oven.

It is a true saying that the fastest way to a man's heart is through his stomach. It is how I won my husband's heart. No kidding. I am totally convinced my shortbread did it (the recipe is a family secret). On an otherwise uneventful New Year's Eve twenty-five years ago he bit into that delectable treat and before it melted in his mouth the look on his face said, "Be mine."

Consequently, I found that good food and home cooking were the consistent and dependable way to his heart. Homemade chicken soup is fail-safe. The stock is boiled from left over cooked chicken, bones, skin, gravy, etc. I add fresh vegetables, brown rice, and my secret herbs and spices. He always comes home for dinner. That is a quality I have learned to appreciate in a man.

My history with the art of cooking, I'm not ashamed to say, is closely tied to my desire to please others. As a card-carrying feminist since I was age seven, I fought for equality with my brothers, but I never once thought it subservient to cook. It is a creative art, satisfying on many levels.

When I brought home rock buns from domestic science class at age twelve, it elicited some rare compliments and appreciation from my taciturn father. That did it!

Soon I began a "baking night" once a week. After about four hours in the kitchen I proudly produced meat pies, coffeecake, apple tarts, and shortbread for the Sunday tea. My mother spent another four hours cleaning up the mess I made, but she didn't seem to mind. On Sunday she proudly invited her friends to the feast, and I got more positive applause for my efforts.

Not that Mum couldn't cook. But it wasn't her favourite. She sported a stout frame that demonstrated to one and all her financial success as a businesswoman as well as her love of fried food. Sunday breakfast was her specialty.

My long-time friends still remember "your Mum's fry-up." If you haven't had a plate of ham and eggs cooked in sizzling lard with sausage, black pudding, fried potato scones, fried tomatoes, and toast with marmalade washed down with a pot of strong Earl Grey then I guess you weren't invited. Sorry.

Cooking for me is about the spontaneous compliments from a father who is uncomfortable giving praise; it's about soothing the crying child; it's about landing the cute guy; it's about sharing with others in the clan the provisions that have been gathered and prepared and presented with love; it's a primitive ritual.

Food and love go together, as do food and memories, or food and family. I will always remember the evocative smells from Mum's kitchen. And I will always remember where all the important family decisions were made. Over the kitchen table, of course. And clinched with a piece of Dundee cake and a pot of tea.

And Granny. Now there was a cook to boast about. I treasure the line from the movie "I Love You to Death."

Tracey Ullman can't do anything right for her Italian mother-in-law. After a wonderful meal she has struggled to prepare, she rattles off all the good things she's put in the recipe. The old lady counters with "In my day we didn't need ingredients."

My granny didn't either. She arrived on Saturdays and took over the kitchen. Even if the larder seemed bare she'd produce something scrumptious for tea … pancakes, scones and sponge cake, and she invariably had a jar of homemade strawberry jam in her shopping bag. Just in case.

Now I'm a granny, and my joy is seeing my grandson with chocolate pudding smeared from ear to ear, deep in thought. "You always make me something with chocolate when I'm here. Don't you, Nana?"

"You betcha'."

And talking about Italian mothers-in-law. I have one, but she never insults my cooking. In fact she loves to come to dinner, and it's not JUST to see her most favourite person in the world, "her wee boy."

My father-in-law, the food critic, paid me the ultimate compliment in three stages:

One: He didn't say one word till he finished the huge plate of pasta with my homemade sauce.

Two: As he used his napkin he wondered aloud how a Scottish girl can make spaghetti sauce.

And three:

Wait for it …

He said it was as good as his mother's.

Those are the kind of compliments that keep a chef happy in her addiction to cooking.

Come Oan Git Aff

Upstairs on the Double

We were brought up near Glasgow, or The Town, as it was referred to in Coatbridge. Private cars were a luxury and certainly not available to a young adult. So travelling by bus was a major part of our social lives. I remember when being allowed to go upstairs on the double-decker without Mum meant you were at a certain age. I'm not sure if it meant that she trusted you to be on your own or if she needed a break.

If it was the first reason, her trust was misplaced because the information, habits, and language you learned on the upper deck were likely to stay with you for life. For good or evil!

Downstairs, the clientele was more genteel. Ladies on weekdays, with their second best hats, sat with the big leather bag on their lap that would be loaded with the day's shopping on the way home. Everyone quietly took in the scenery as if in awe ... Coatbridge to Glasgow, mind. But upstairs in the smoke-filled noisy quarter, people talked out loud, and on a lap you might see a favoured racing dog. Men were protective of their Whippets. He might win tonight. And the back seat, generally reserved for courting couples, was always occupied on a Friday or Saturday. With the rest of the passengers facing forward you might be able to steal a kiss.

For a child, riding on the bus offers basic training for life. Some examples: finding a shelter in the rain while you wait; figuring out your route; catching the right bus; having money available for your fare; choosing your seat with care; knowing where your stop is and being ready to disembark. All of these have consequences for travelling across town and for life in general. And, when you're old enough to be out that late, knowing when the last bus leaves is vital.

Getting to the bus stop on time was probably a kid's first difficult lesson on planning. When the big green Baxter's bus from Blairhill pulls out at 8:30 and you're not on it, you will be late for school at Coatbridge High. In my case it was: "Oh no, not again!" Being on time is a harder lesson for some.

The conductress, part ticket taker, part policewoman, part Mum, patrolled the bus regularly to collect fares, always returning, like a sentry, to the platform to direct traffic: "Come oan get aff !" she'd yell at any passenger who was kind of slow on the disembark.

Or to move the crowd of schoolchildren off the platform she'd yell, "Upstairs on the double."

We resisted. As young girls, squealing, were pushed ahead by voyeuristic young studs hanging back to go last up the stairs after the girls. C'mon, guys. Admit it. Girls all wore skirts back then, remember.

The conductress kept her eyes skint for freeloaders sitting, feigning innocence, and ignoring the "Clippie" calling out "fares please" and making the "ching-ching" noises on her ticket punch up and down the aisle, You hoped she'd think you had a ticket already, and it might save you a sixpence, but the weight of guilt on your Calvinistic or Catholic conscience did have costs. The shame of it could cause distraction that might be carried through to second period at school and result in you attracting negative attention from the teacher.

Then again it might not. Sixpence bought shame-defying treats at Bessie's wee sweetie shop on the corner.

There were words, Bad Wurrds, heard especially on a Friday or Saturday night that I never heard at home, and knew that it would be unwise to try them out there. And raucous songs that supported your particular affiliations to the Blue or the Green, the Rangers or the Celtic, the Scots or the Irish that could cause disharmony and could result in an inebriated balladeer being expelled from the bus. But those were rare occasions. Etiquette upstairs was far more broad-minded than the rules that affected behaviour down below.

Riding on the lower level, you were exposed to polite society and all the rules that pertained at that time. Even the seats were arranged differently so that you were obliged, proud even, to give up your seat to a standing elderly person or someone holding a baby. Chalk up your good deed for the day. People spoke quietly, if at all, to the person sitting next to them. It was a great opportunity to share, or overhear, stories. If you had a snack, it would most likely be from a wee white poke of caramels produced discreetly from a handbag or a pocket and maybe even shared with the person sitting next to you.

Upstairs you could enjoy, without embarrassment, a poke of chips dripping with malt vinegar or even a full fish supper and a bottle of Irn Bru and, of course, a smoke.

That coming of age tradition; that great divider of the men from the boys—the self-confident, cigarette-smoking women from the girls, the ubiquitous fag, Woodbine, five in a pack. I couldn't wait to learn how. Then I had to figure out how to smoke all five before going home, because smoking was a sin, and without getting sick. Waste not; want not.

At sixteen I found a teacher, a girl just a few years older and very sophisticated. She taught me how to inhale without choking. A valuable lesson I carried for twenty plus years until I learned what I should have learned from the sign downstairs: NO SMOKING.

Choosing the back seat on the top of the bus allowed a certain amount of privacy and, if you chose it on a Saturday night with a young lad in tow, you might get kissed. If you led him to the front where you were more visible, he was being warned to behave. If you led him to the downstairs, he was on his last legs.

There are very few buses where I live in Florida, and I wonder: How do children learn life's important lessons, the ones from upstairs and the ones from downstairs?

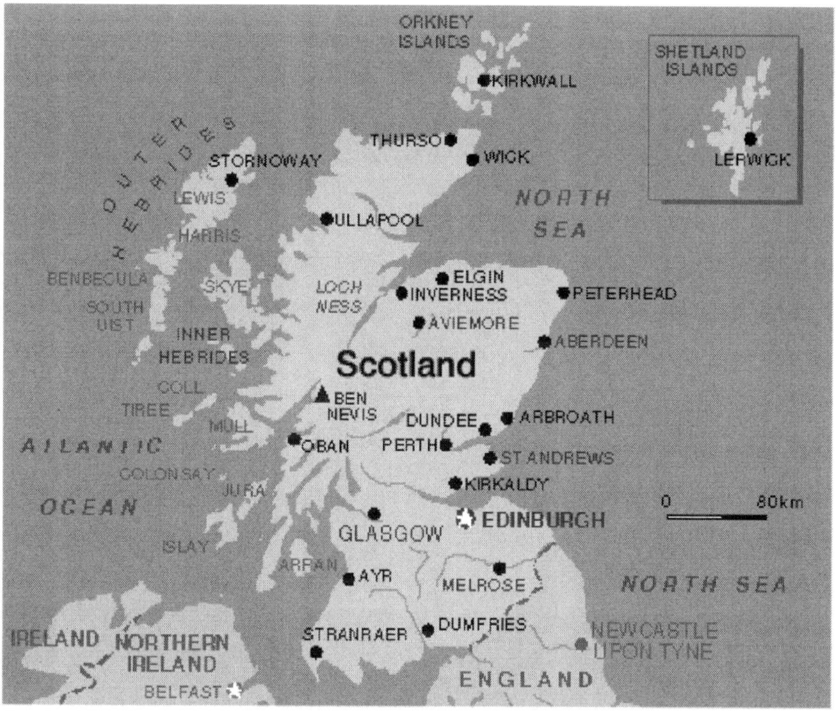
ORKNEY ISLANDS
KIRKWALL
SHETLAND ISLANDS
LERWICK
OUTER HEBRIDES
STORNOWAY
THURSO
WICK
LEWIS
HARRIS
ULLAPOOL
NORTH SEA
BENBECULA
SOUTH UIST
SKYE
LOCH NESS
ELGIN
INVERNESS
PETERHEAD
AVIEMORE
ABERDEEN
INNER HEBRIDES
Scotland
COLL
TIREE
BEN NEVIS
MULL
DUNDEE
ARBROATH
ATLANTIC
OBAN
PERTH
ST ANDREWS
COLONSAY
JURA
KIRKALDY
OCEAN
GLASGOW
EDINBURGH
0
80km
ISLAY
ARRAN
AYR
MELROSE
NORTH SEA
IRELAND
NORTHERN IRELAND
STRANRAER
DUMFRIES
NEWCASTLE UPON TYNE
BELFAST
ENGLAND

John and Shari Milne's wedding at Mount Dora, Florida.

Travelling Back in Time

Say Wha'?

Then there is the hazard, when visiting abroad, of being perceived as an American. Well maybe it's not a hazard, but it is awkward when I'm on Princes Street and someone assumes the responsibility, however kindly, to educate me about my native land. "That's the castle up there on the hill."

"Thank you," I answer with enthusiasm.

Now, I've enjoyed visits to Edinburgh Castle since I was a wee lass, but I still stand in awe at the impressive fortifications, just like any tourist. I can still remember feeling the stillness creep over me as I stood in the tiny chapel in the centre of that majestic edifice when I was about the same age as the girl Queen Margaret who sought solace there back in the 13th century.

Looking over the battlements to the New Town, I am mesmerized.

"Is this your first trip over?" The inquiry is perfectly friendly so I hate to embarrass the young woman.

"Actually, I was born here."

"Oh. Ye've lost yer accent."

What to say? I really haven't lost my accent; I remember where I put it, and I found it again when I had the opportunity to read the famous Robert Burns' poem "Tam 'o Shanter" at the Dunedin Reader's Festival recently, in Florida ... just in time.

I've lived here longer than I lived in Bonnie Scotland, and I'm afraid I sound more like an American (except to Americans, who say, "Love your accent. What is it?").

I'm neither "fish nor fowl" in the accent department. I like to say, in my defence, that I can be understood anywhere the English language is spoken.

This was very important when I arrived in Michigan, where I worked as a nurse, several decades ago. My skills were more than adequate, being a proud graduate of the prestigious Glasgow Royal Infirmary School of Nursing! Of course, you'd expect the rest of the world to understand a perfectly satisfactory West of Scotland tongue spoken slowly and deliber-r-r-rately, but I soon learned that my communication style needed modification and my burr needed softening, as my patients were American weans.

I'm not sure how much comfort they took from, "Och, ye'll be fine. Don't greet. Wheesht! Here's a wee sweetie," if they didn't understand it.

But ... when I said, "Stay still. I'm just goin' tae give ye a wee jag," they were totally unprepared and outraged at the pain that was delivered to their innocent wee bottoms. SO. I learned to say, "Take the medicine and you'll get this candy," and, "Hold still, this li'l shot isn't gonna' hurt." I became "bilingual" through compassionate necessity.

Many years of participation in community theatre further developed my dialect variations, but no matter how carefully I wrap my tongue around it, my pronunciations of "look," "book," "took," and especially "food" don't sound right on either side of the pond anymore.

In my defence, the word "toe-may-toe" has never passed my lips, and I can still say, "It's a braw, bricht moonlit nicht the nicht."

To add to my Scots resume: My shortbread is famous. I

can concoct a pot of soup out of practically any ingredients AND I like haggis. Honest.

Since I started writing Scottish historical fiction several years ago, my Scots accent is becoming more discernible (according to my American-born daughter). I guess walking around all day fantasizing 19th century Highland and Lowland conversations might be the cause.

A trip to Scotland this year, and a Scottish family wedding here in Florida, steeped me in a rich mixture of Glaswegian and Aberdonian and has probably placed my mid-Atlantic accent somewhere east of Greenland.

Ah couldn't believe my eyes!

What would a Scottish book be without a picture of highland cattle!

The Hazards of Driving in Scotland

The U.S. travel agents promised that our car insurance would cover the use of a vehicle in Scotland. We arrived at the car rental counter in Glasgow airport at 7 a.m. Greenwich Mean Time that September morning, which was in conflict with my circadian cycle which has been on Eastern Standard Time these many years. It was 2 a.m. Let's face it; I was crabbit, and my husband was basically sleepwalking.

Certainly not prepared for the sandy-haired Amazon from Paisley who, in no uncertain terms, informed us that we had to pay insurance in the amount of ... how many pounds? Tell me again. It sounded like the same amount we had shelled out for the actual car rental.

Paul, probably thinking he needed to find the way out of a bad dream where this brawny lass, who probably held her own with six older brothers, would jump the counter and relieve him of said pounds while inflicting mythic pain, said, "Pay her."

We were stunned, but we had a vehicle and now faced the challenge of negotiating Glesca' traffic and beyond to the green hills that would warm my heart.

After so many years of living and driving in America, motoring on the left-hand side of the road is now unfamiliar—and definitely not for the faint-hearted. We learned that the routes with the ominous warning "No

Caravans Allowed," always seemed to lead to the most picturesque places but gave us the most heart-stopping driving moments. Driving on the left-hand side of ancient narrow drove roads with white lines down the middle; roads that were used by Rob Roy and his caterans, is downright hazardous. But I was ecstatic to be touring my beloved Scottish Highlands.

"Unfamiliar" was not the word my husband, Paul, used to describe the transportation experience on his first visit a couple of years ago. He never offered to take over the driving, mind you, wouldn't even attempt it. Terrifying, he called it. He rode shotgun and, offered helpful suggestions along the way. Like:

"What the hell are you doing?"

And. "Let me out at the next stop."

Or "Did you see how close you came to that guy's rearview mirror?"

These are the comments fit to print.

Between Glasgow and Aberdeen, he witnessed the art of negotiating roundabouts (from someone who hadn't used them in decades).

"Watch out; you're too close to the kerb."

How he knew that, with his eyes covered, I'll never know.

From Inverurie (which is the only Scottish word he learned) we headed to Tomintoul on what the map defined as the "Highland Tourist Route."

I drove, awed by the sights and, for the most part, oblivious to his terror. The roads that cling to the edge of the mountains offer the best views.

"Look at the heather. Och, it's lovely."

Him. "What happens if we meet another car?"

"Nae bother. The Scots are very polite."

Then I thought, maybe there's some other reason they're getting out of my way!

"See the Highland cattle; the ones with the long shaggy coats."

"You're going over the e-e-e-edge."

I never tire of the craggy, sheep-dotted Hielands, the mountaintops shrouded in mist, and the glens that change shades from almost black to delicate green in response to shadows created by the scudding clouds. Scottish skies are never boring. They change like a kaleidoscope; never clear blue as some foreign skies are; never one shade of grey or purple or green either.

Monet in the Grampians.

In my reverie I must have swerved then.

"Aaargh!"

I'd almost forgotten I had a passenger.

Descending into farm country, I am filled, as always, with wonder at the miles and miles of dykes, like strings of rare grey pearls, luminescent with silvered lichen. Noble stone edifices bound to renew our respect for our forebears, who dragged every rock out of the peaty soil to form those enduring walls, then were forced to leave, in the thousands, when the land wouldn't sustain them, or the devastating approach of "progress" drove them off.

We stayed overnight in Aviemore in a B&B, making another fortunate choice. Driving around, I got to practice my parallel parking, (not what my husband called it). An automobile enthusiast, he checked the car out frequently and reported to me (yet again) that the left rear hubcap was taking a beating. I refused to believe this despite the evidence. I must have been coming too close to the kerbs, perhaps over-correcting in order to prevent possible collisions.

Aviemore proved to be more cosmopolitan than I had expected, but the piper in full highland regalia playing in front of the Cairngorm Hotel thrilled me and fascinated my husband.

Then on to Kingussie to the Highland Folk Museum, where I wanted to do research for my novel, *My Blood Is Royal*, which is set in the 19th century, and was born of my fascination with Auld Scotland and its hardy folks. Inside the authentic old "Blackhouse," we marvelled at the stone structure, a "full-service" building which, within its tight space, housed a byre for the cattle, an entryway that accommodated the hens and to your right the fire room where the family lived, dimly lit by a small window, and one adjacent bedroom.

The ancient stones that protected our forebears from the wintry blast still held the chill from the last ice age. Soot from the fire in the middle of the room painted ghostly images on the walls before it escaped through a hole in the thatch. A modern-day lass with a bad cold sat dressed in period costume, huddled around the fire, and it was August. We, spoiled by central heating, got chilled to the bone within ten minutes. The setting evoked images of the highland mother making scones on the girdle and conjured the aroma of a big kettle of kale, fragrant with onions, bubbling over the fire and the womenfolk lined up on one side of the fire and the men on the other waiting, bowls in hand for their plain meal.

I made mental photographs of that and other such scenes that occurred to me, and couldn't wait to get back to my writing to describe them while they were still fresh.

For now, it's back into our rental car for another breathtaking driving adventure. We were headed to Pitlochrie, and a reunion with old friends now living in Canada: other expatriate Scots visiting the auld sod.

We have one more week to soak up Scotland's beauty; then it's time to cross the pond. But first, we have to return the rental car.

The dawn stick-up for additional insurance, at Glasgow Airport, now a dim memory, I waited in the shuttle while Paul went into the shop-front office to return the rental car. My usually, but not always, mild-mannered Italian husband exploded out of there about fifteen minutes later. He had a look I recognized, best described as understudy for Al

Pacino after he's made an offer that can't be refused.

"What happened?"

"Insurance problem." Understatement. "He said the insurance didn't cover the damage to the hubcap."

"Oops. What did you do?"

"I asked him if the insurance would cover backing up the damned car into his plate glass window."

Over-reaction? I didn't think so.

Despite his trepidation, my travelling companion swears he'll be back.

Och! We're no awa' tae bide awa'.

A Hielan' Coo

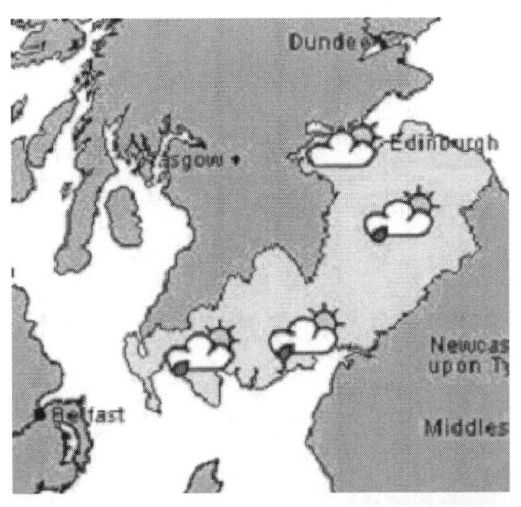

A Wee Bit Rain Cannae Stop the Lassies

Rainstorming

I read one time that the Inuit have thirty words for snow. Och, that's nothing! We Scots have at least that many for RAIN.

I needed that many wurrds and a few more on my recent trip to my homeland. When we left Inverness in the morning the sun shone, but by the time we reached Fort William it was gie drumlie or awful gloomy. We then drove through the infamous Glencoe and felt about as vulnerable as a bunch of MacDonalds entertaining a band of treacherous Campbells. It was lashin' or evendoon as in: heavy, continuous rain, falling straight, perpendicular. Instant waterfalls poured out and off the mountain. Imagine making your escape out of that valley, through the bracken in a rain-soaked kilt and wool socks.

I blessed the vintage car my old friend, Beryl, drove that threw up a spray ahead and around it and kept on going. I never saw rain like that before. Surrounding us, a torrent of water ran in white rivulets down the mountain like lace curtains pulled to shut out a dreich afternoon. The gullies and burns were level with the road. We had to use a recently constructed diversion ahead where the road had washed out. Later we learned that the rain on that day had set a twenty-four-year record.

Even if you've never heard broad Scots spoken before, the words for rain have to evoke a response if not a rejoinder.

Discussion of the weather is de rigueur in the Scottish lexicon of good manners. It's the "opening line" for any social situation. Our primary form of greeting for friends and strangers alike is generally a comment about the weather. And of the weather much can be said.

Some comments invite response and have, no doubt, been the salutation that began new friendships, like "Terrible weather for the Glasgow Fair, is it not?'

"Aye, terrible." Sizing up the accent (foreign) and the friendly visitor's naivety, the polite response is, "Ye've never been tae Rothesay before then, eh?"

Other weather comments serve to hail a neighbour.

"A wee bit damp oot, eh?"

Or

"Threatenin' all afternoon, was it no'?"

"Aye. It was overcast till teatime, then the rain came on."

Or

"Wouldn't ye know, fine dryin' weather and it's not my washin' day."

"Good day to do your windows, though."

"Och, I'm not botherin'. Ye cannae keep them clean anyway."

Weather conversations can deftly lead to sports conversations, especially around Glasgow.

"Och, looks like rain again. Have ye noticed Setterdays are aye like this when the Rangers have a big game?"

One-upmanship is acceptable and it's even polite to get in the last word when discussing weather.

"Nice outside the day. Is it not?"

"Aye, if the rain stays away."

But since it often doesn't stay away, we Scots have expanded the language for wet weather way beyond the usual English expressions for rain. Words like cloudburst, precipitation, squall, shower, downpour, torrent, blustery or even "coming doon cats and dugs" are fine but do they really paint a picture? Can you feel it dripping down the back of your neck? Does it help you to smell the pervading dampness?

Not on your Nellie!

Travel around Scotland and listen for the friendly weather reports from people who know their weather. There are onomatopoetic words you'll hear only in and around Lanarkshire.

For example, in Glasgow, if it's warsh, you'd better find a warm jacket. If it's mistin', drizzlin', sprinklin', spittin,' patterin,' or jist a smirr, take a light raincoat. On the other hand, if it's drenchin', or pourin' doon in buckets, or even worse, in stair rods, wait a wee while indoors.

Only the verbally challenged in Glasgow would say that the rain is "falling." Rain isn't simply falling. No! It's threatenin', drivin', peltin', stoatin' aff the road, streamin', pourin' or teemin'.

If you go out in the rain you'll not only get wet; you could get soakin' wet, drippin' wet, soppin' wet, wringin' wet, soaked, drencht or droont.

In some parts of the country showers are subdivided into sun showers, wee showers and skurrachs (wee fast showers), or thunder-plumps (sudden heavy, noisy showers). Which is frightening enough, but say you're in Banff and you hear a local say, "It's bullet-stanes out there." Obviously you'd stay inside. Right?

In Aberdeen if it's a drabble, you might get a little wet, but if it's bleatery or plowtery outside, stay by the fire. For any other kind of weather conversation in Aberdeen get an interpreter. The same advice applies for Orkney.

I had the pleasure of visiting in Banff, in Aberdeenshire, with a local native during a weather event.

A friendly stranger waylaid us as we struggled to stay vertical in the gale. "Blin' drift," he sez.

"A fierce blizzard where visibility is zero," my interpreter told me, then responded. "Aye aye, mochie day. Hale watter." She yells the translation into my ear, "Heaviest rain possible."

"Bla' the spokes fae the posties's bike." This guy wasn't going to give up. He was a "last word" kind of Scot.

I have only touched the tip of the iceberg with this brainstorm about weather. Is it merely a tempest in a teapot or a subject open to a storm of controversy?

I expect a deluge of reaction and a hailstorm of protest from Scots whose favourite words have been left out in the rain.

Have a nice day.

Brave Hearts Are Not Worn on the Sleeve

I am trying here to disprove the conventional wisdom that Scottish men are not romantic.

I talked to my Scottish friend in Canada about the possibilities of writing a bit about how Scots express their feelings. "Hmph-Hmph," she said, "That'll be easy and short. They don't."

Can that be true?

I'll pose my question and most of the substance of this treatise to the lassies, because it is primarily you canny ScotsMEN who bear the brunt of the reputation of being "no' that romantic."

You see, I'd like to put to rest the theory that Scots are reticent to show feelings. And I am starting with the controversial issue of Romantic Love and the Scot. I mean, do we have to leave it all to Robert Burns to express?

You say, "But he did it so well." And someone adds "And so often." In fact he was a fella who could get himself into more trouble expressing feelings than Errol Flynn or Clark Gable or any other Lothario who comes to mind.

Yes, the bard's reputation for "womanizing" on a grand scale was something he didn't bother to hide.

Leaving aside any judgment on his social behaviour, I think we can all agree he had an uncanny ability to express his sensitivity in ways that touch our hearts.

Ae fond kiss, and then we sever
Ae fareweel, alas forever!
Deep in heart-wrung tears I'll pledge thee
Warring sighs and groans I'll pledge thee

How do we explain the deeply feeling, moving words of Rabbie (a pure Scot)? He addresses Patriotism, Grieving, Death, and Romantic Love; to name a few.

Even without a total familiarity of the Auld Scots Tongue most Scots (and others) will understand the passion and the beauty in the verse.

As a child, I remember my father reading Burns to us in the evening and always he'd get the lump in his throat. Come to think of it, it might not have been the sentimental, romantic verses that were to blame.

I can hear his trembling baritone:

Now's the day and, now's the hour:
See the front of battle lour!
See approach proud Edward's power –
Chains and slaverie!

That's what did it. Images of tough men scantily dressed in colourful attire, coming over the hill, emitting blood-curdling screams and brandishing assorted primitive weapons. It'll make ye tear up quicker'n peelin' an onion.

Does the object of your desire; your appointed Valentine, your Scottish lover, have Burns' romantic style lurking in his heart? Does your wee man have a passionate, loving tender impractical streak?

Right away you answer "No." You think he could never compare to:

And fare thee weel, my only love,
And fare thee weel awhile!
And I will come again my love

Tho' it were ten thousand miles.

But, wait. Burns is talking about lost love. Ending a relationship. Unattainable love. Love of the unrequited variety. Now that is something different. *Parting is such sweet sorrow*, says the OTHER poet.

Easy to get teary eyed about the depth of your love when she's walking out the door.

"Och. Yer no leavin' me are ye! Ah'm over here greetin'."

I am reminded of a scene I witnessed at Glasgow Central years ago.

"I'm off to Canada," says the lad who has obviously spent the previous hours accepting parting libations or potions from friends. One young lass seems particularly moved. Apparently on her behalf, he breaks out in a World War II song:

"Goodbye, Dolly, I am leaving
Tho' it breaks ma heart to go."

The singer here is doing a sort of "Highland Fling" to the melody. His achy-breaky heart is across the ocean already.

Ah! Faithless love.

Perhaps you're just not paying enough attention to your guy's subtlety. Don't look for the flowery variety of courtship. If it shows up it will be obvious. You know what I mean ... the ostentatious bouquet, the garment in red satin that might have fitted you ten years ago, the candlelight dinner with the hovering, unobtrusive waiter, the ride home in a hired horse drawn carriage.

This may not happen.

"Did ye hurt yersel'?" on stubbing your toe or some other painful event may be the closest you get. Or perhaps: "Gie's a wee cheaper." Unsubtle foreplay.

Maybe it's the harsh climate, or the struggle to survive as a people, or maybe we are just taciturn, reserved, aloof, quiet by nature, reserved, reticent, introverted, etc. Whatever it is, our menfolk keep their cards pretty close to the vest.

Except Valentine's cards!

So I ran the question past Jimsy on my cut-rate long distance phone service from the USA today. It is a very nasty cold day in Balfron. It has been raining for twenty-four hours straight and the adjacent field is flooded. He is cozied up to a fire and relaxed in the comfort of a very long-term marriage that has, long ago, worked out any kinks.

He waxed philosophical. "Aye." He agreed with the adjectives I had used. They described his own attitude. "It's the weather. The climate forces you indoors and you're there thegither. Location-wise, ye're captive." Despite the inescapable inevitability in his words, there was more than acceptance here; there was tenderness, caring and an unspoken "I wouldn't want it any other way."

"So," I says, "the climate creates forced intimacy, and in this family crucible lasting relationships are forged."

"Aye"

Now for the specifics. "How is this togetherness expressed; say at Valentine's Day?"

"No. I've never sent my wife a Valentine. And probably your brothers never did either."

I had to agree. The thought of any of my brothers picking out a wee flowery card with hearts on it is almost laughable.

UNLESS they could find one that said something like:

"Did ye hurt yersel'?"

OR

"UR YE AW RIGHT, HEN?"

Very subtle ... you have to watch for it.

Post Script: My niece Fiona, my brother's daughter, was visiting me and after reading this said, "You know, he did give my mother a card once and a bunch of flowers even."

This took my breath away until she added, "When Mum had me on February 14th. Yes, that's my birthday. That was the only time, I think."

Aunt Nan's Secret Shortbread Recipe:

Good butter 1/2 lb
Superfine Sugar 1/4 lb (1/2 cup)
Flour 1 lb (3 cups plain flour. 1 cup rice flour or cornstarch)
Salt ½ Teaspoon

Preparation:

Put on your favourite CD of Scottish ballads and sing along. This definitely helps.

I used to make a pile of the flour and sugar and carefully knead the butter into it. This is traditional and takes a little practice.

Now I use my food processor to cream the butter and sugar. I then incorporate about ½ of the flour into the creamed butter and sugar still using the (illegal) machine.

Then it is emptied onto a clean flat surface and as much of the remaining flour as you can work into it is kneaded to a stiff consistency. This is as authentic as Aunt Nan made but with a little less work.

Roll it out with a rolling pin to about ½ inch.

Shape in the traditional wheel, prick all over the top with a fork and pinch the edges.

–OR–

I use a "cookie" cutter now and it makes about 2 dozen shortbread "cookies" (you can invent your own shapes or cut it into fingers.) Prick all over with a fork.

Into a 325 degree oven for about 20 mins.
Check often. It should be golden.
Sprinkle with castor sugar before it cools.
Cool on a wire rack.
Hide in sealed tin till Hogmanay.
Good luck with the hiding part.

I dare you!

The Hazards of Scottish Food

There were modern eating hazards, I discovered on my recent trips to Scotland; hazards that went beyond the temptations of scones and chocolate biscuits served with frequent cups of tea; new temptations in the land of porridge and potatoes.

My husband, who was raised in New York, has acquired a taste for Scottish soups after this many years of marriage to a Scot. So, imagine our delight when, visiting in Callander, we found a wee shop that served soup exclusively, huge tureens of steaming Scotch broth and potato soup redolent of leeks.

On his second visit to the restaurant he was unsupervised, as I was off doing research at the Rob Roy Museum. Now, I know New York can be a tough city where you have to be able to take care of yourself, but put a hungry Yank, with no education about the strict British etiquette of queuing, in a "soup kitchen" and watch out.

He says that he accidentally put himself ahead in the line in front of two Scottish matrons in stout brogues and tweed skirts who looked like they'd trekked over the moors all morning and had worked up an appetite.

Queuing in the U.K. is more than standing in line, or even waiting your turn, as any eight-year-old schoolchild can tell you. It is a complex formula of rules and etiquette. It might even be a law. It is certainly one of those situations where ignorance of the rule is not an excuse. Some places in the U.S. you'll see signs "Line Starts Here," or "Take a Number," causing great consternation in the average American.

Queuing does not require signs or even conversation usually. We Brits just form a regimented column. Nae problem! There are extenuating circumstances that call for limited conversation, e.g., accidentally getting ahead in a line requires, no, demands, an enthusiastic apology. "So terribly sorry." — "Didn't see you there."

So I realized the Yank had probably committed some serious queue infraction he might not even be aware of.

He attempted to describe to me the debacle.

He followed his nose, and walked right up to the counter and placed his order oblivious of anyone else. Big mistake! One of the most "memorable moments" of his trip was the enjoyment of the soup and the lesson in Scottish etiquette. When he told me he ordered TWO bowls of soup ahead of the ladies, I was afraid to hear more and told him how closely he had courted disaster.

"I see." But he didn't.

"What did they do?" I asked.

"They stepped back and stood there talking to each other. One said something like 'Whisatyankuptae?'" Which he thought was some kind of greeting. So he smiled at the ladies while he ordered his second bowl. Then: "Leavsumferuswillye?" they said.

At that point he heard the note of sarcasm and thought he might be "out of line."

"Sorry, ladies, did I get ahead of you?"

"Itsaqueuedjit."

"Thank you."

"Hesgotabrassnecksohehas."

When I translated, he was appropriately chastened. That democratic queuettiquette is an institution that New Yorkers could benefit from emulating.

Knowwhitamean?

Another hazard, I found, is to tell your Scottish hostess about the foods you really miss as an expat. I mentioned: meringues, shortbread, and black pudding to name a few. Courtesy of the fabulous Scottish generosity, these treats magically appeared, sometimes at the next meal. Talk aboot yer hazards. My weight and cholesterol rose faster than the U.S. deficit.

The new, improved cuisine in Scotland is not what I remember when I was a lass. Real "fish and chips" is a rarity, and it's hard to find a good plate of mince and tatties. But my cousins, definite gourmets, who live in Balfron, took me to many first class restaurants jist roon the corner from their home. I admit I enjoyed the wonderful curries and authentic Italian food and, of course, a "just for old time's sake" lunch at the Rogano in Glasgow with my cousin, Anne. Risotto to die for. We weren't counting calories.

I must applaud the re-emergence of the Haggis in the homeland. When I was a child, it seemed the (practically extinct) animal only appeared at Burns' suppers and was rarely on the table at home, but through strict conservation methods, the Haggis population has apparently recovered and is increasing, so much so that the tasty dish is re-appearing on menus and grocery shelves all the way from the border up to John 'O Groats. It's a meal guaranteed to stay solidly with you and fight pangs of hunger for long periods of time on treks across the moors or down Sauchiehall Street.

My son-in-law tells me it is not allowed to be imported to the USA. Haggis banned from these Yoonided States? Please, tell me it isn't true. I mean, these folks eat hot dogs!

It was an incident with Scottish food that brought aforesaid husband and me together some twenty-five years ago.

It was a cold winter's night in Northern New York, by the St. Lawrence River, (stop me if I've told you this before) where "COLD" has different parameters than other parts of the lower forty-eight states. As was my custom, I ploughed through the snow on my mission of mercy to deliver boxes of homemade shortbread to friends and acquaintances.

I just happened to be in his neighbourhood, and barely knew him, but he was good-looking and I was single and I had an extra box of shortbread …

Oh! You've heard it.

Going Home

I may never go back to Coatbridge, Lanarkshire, my hometown, again.

No, I can't. Because it's not what it used to be.

Back in the day, it was a dirty, noisy place, dubbed the "Iron Burgh," dominated by iron foundries and coal mines. It still contained several areas of substandard housing left over from the early industrial revolution and tolerated through the dark days of the world wars. A picture of the Rosehall Rows was used for the cover of George Orwell's, *The Road to Wigan Pier*, which describes the dismal living conditions of the working poor of the last century, many of them Irish immigrants. Coatbridge was a boiling cauldron of secular conflict where Catholics and Protestants traditionally lived parallel lives.

Separate schools, separate neighbourhoods and, of course, separate religious institutions. Now, in retrospect, one side attributes the cause of the several hundred-year-old conflict to the other side. Whatever the reasons, separate we were, back in the day.

The Catholics wanted to make religion available in their schools, so children of each faith growing up in the same town were raised as strangers. No mixing.

The Protestants gave favoured job assignments to other Protestants, so the Catholics had a struggle out of poverty, retaining the status quo. There were many other reasons that the divisions between the sects were broadly accepted and kept in place. Way too complicated for me, as a young person at the time, to understand.

Forty odd years ago, my cousin Gordon, who, like me, had been raised in a Protestant fundamentalist tradition (our grandfather was master of that most anti-catholic organization, the Grand Orange Lodge of Scotland, purported "to promote the great ideals of Protestantism and Liberty," for goodness sake), married his Catholic sweetheart. Gordon and Kathleen lived and raised a fine family and conducted a successful business within the confines of this "most Irish" town in Scotland. Brave lad and lassie.

No, I may never go back to Coatbridge because I want to preserve the memory of my last recent visit.

It was a sunny, cool day, that Friday of the September weekend 2008. I asked my cousin, Anne, to take me to the "Fountain," a tall, granite landmark and rendezvous spot at the heart of the town, the crossroads of five intersecting streets.

"Meet me at the Fountain," was the start of many a budding romance. My aunt's hardware store, which was in our family for generations, is gone and a florist, with a colourful, artistic window display, has taken its place. I saw men, at least one Scotsman, walking about with a bouquet of flowers. It looked very manly, in case you are wondering. We bought flowers to take to the Old Monkland Cemetery to put on the graves of our many relatives honoured with stone monuments there.

From the Fountain up Main Street the area is a pedestrian-only shopping area dominated by the elegant façade of St. Patrick's Catholic Church. An arc of steps invites the faithful to take a moment from earthly endeavours to climb up and speak to God.

Coatbridge Fountain
Where friends met up

The last time I went to St. Patrick's was a few years ago to attend the funeral of my Cousin Gordon's wife, Kathleen, who died, sadly, in mid-life. It was an amazing day. The funeral turned out to be the most heartening meeting and sharing of Catholics and Protestants grieving a mutual friend. It was standing room only.

Now, years later, my cousin Anne and I were moved to go into the church to remember the moment and honour her.

That's when we met Father Eamon in the entryway. He stood in all his glory in white flowing attire and on his robe was emblazoned a gold stitched image of Jesus and Mary. A shock of white hair topped his ruddy smiling face, but it was his eyes that caught my attention: piercing blue with a steady gaze. You would never dream of telling a lie to that face, and you would never fear of telling the truth. The lilt of Ireland lent music to his voice as he welcomed us. It was obvious we didn't know our way around. We explained our connection, and he had known my cousin's wife well. We could still hear the loss of her in his voice.

When we left, he saw us out and stood at the top of the impressive stairs surveying his flock.

On this beautiful day the town seemed to be in a festive mood as though Central Casting, Inc. had sent an array of happy villagers out in their holiday finery to add life to the village square.

The baker's shop had people spilling out into the street. I looked in the window and, I swear, those were the self-same cakes and tea bread my mother served on Saturdays a half century ago. The butcher shop was likewise crowded. I wondered if the sausages were as meaty and spicy as I remember. I haven't had a decent sausage since I came to America. People were shopping for their weekend. Everybody seemed to know everybody else. I looked for a familiar face, but it had been a long time.

We went into a shop for a cup of delicious coffee. There were several places to eat. When I was a girl there was only Coia's Ice-cream Parlour (homemade, and served in a cone or on a wafer. For the hearty appetite there was double nougat), and a couple of fish 'n chip places (sadly missed). But that was it, and if you wanted coffee you made your own with hot milk and Nestlé's crystals or Camp coffee. I remember that thick brown stuff flavoured with chicory.

Caught up in the festivities, we did a wee bit of shopping too. I found an outfit that fit me like the skin of a haggis. I must be the same size and shape as quite a few other Scottish women.

Some things never change.

Grannie's Scones
(Rhymes with bygones)

Black-lead the stove the day afore because ye cannae do it when it's bakin' day.

Start a good fire right after yer man leaves for work. Ye'll know when it's hot enough for baking scones, ye have tae open the window

Recipe:

Tak' aboot six haunfu's o' flour
add a spoon o' bakin' powder
and two spoons o' sugar
and a good pinch o' salt in a bowl.

Cut a good nub o' butter intae it and work with yer fingers to the consistency o' bread crumbs.

Add a beaten egg and enough milk off the top 'o the bottle and stir in, just till it wants tae stick tae the sides o' the bowl.

Stir in a wee haunfu' o' currants.

Now watch how I do the rest of it, she sez.

I think the dough was rolled out to about half an inch thick, cut in wedges and brushed with beaten egg white. But it all happened so fast I can't swear to it.

(Sorry, that's it. You're on your own.)

But they were really good.

Serve with homemade strawberry jam and Devonshire cream.

*Robert Fox, my grandfather,
the Patriarch*

Tall Tales My Grandfather Told Us

Sunday at Grandpa's

Sunday at Grandpa's was a break we looked forward to, an entertaining event that relieved the monotonous duty of the multiple church attendances that were expected of us children.

My brothers and I hurried over to Grandpa and Grandma's house after the Sunday morning service, for lunch and treats and surreptitious readings of the Dandy and the Beano comics and, of course, Grandpa's stories.

"Did I ever tell you about the time ma horse went intae the chapel and drank the Holy Watter?"

The correct answer was "No."

And we were off …!

He pulled out his Meerschaum pipe and his pouch and stuffed a nest of tobacco into the bowl, patted it down carefully, then lit a taper from the roaring fire in the grate, touched it to the white clay pipe, and sucked hard about three times before blowing out an admirable cloud of pungent smoke.

"Ou-Aye. That's when I was in business for maself. Afore I'd started they stores. I had a fine horse and a cairt with a sign painted on the side, 'Purveyor of Goods.'

"Yon Tam was the smartest horse in Whifflet … maybe

in the whole o' Lanarksheer. Och, the truth is, there wisnae a finer Clydesdale in Scotland. He could back up a close nae bother and never scrape the walls or dunt the cairt. Back up, mind ye. Smart, smart auld cuddy. Ou-aye, I still miss that horse. Yer faither liked him too. How do ye think he grew the best roses in Whifflet? Auld Tam left his callin' card every day outside his door. Wheeched it aff the road, ontae the garden, did John."

"Grandpa, about the horse …"

"Ou-Aye. Well I was getting back from ma rounds one Setterday, and Auld Tam had a loose shoe, so I made straight for Davy's blacksmith shop on Hozier Street.

"'Rab Fox, it's yourself, is it?' he says.

"'Aye,' ah telt him, 'Tam's ready to throw aff another shoe. Have ye the time tae fix it?'

"'This job I'm ontae will be another hour or so. Do ye want to wait, Rab?'

"'Would ye mind if I left him here and went roon the corner? I'm in need of something to wet my whistle afore it dries up and blaws away.'

"'Aye, right ye are, Rab,' he says. 'Come back in an hour and a half. It's three o'clock; I close at five.'"

We watched in awe while Grandpa cleared his throat and took aim for the highly polished brass spittoon. He never missed. It was a perfect rim shot that rang out into the room in the key of E sharp. He waited for the reverberation to subside before continuing.

"So ah hurried up the street to the shelter of the Big Tree Bar, put ma foot on the brass rail and laid down a shilling. 'How drunk can I get for that?' says I to the publican.

"'For you, Rab, this and another one like it should do.' Bartenders are aye fast wi' the wisecracks. He pulled a pint and poured a dram of whisky to go with it."

(At that moment in the storytelling, my grandma, a former officer in the Salvation Army, and devoted temperance advocate, returned to the room. This critical audience required him making some adjustment to his tale.)

"Now you weans have tae remember, this all happened before ah found the Lord. Yer grandma showed me the error of ma ways lang syne. Och, Ah havenae had a drap since ah don't know when." His eyes had a longing, far-away look that confirmed his sincerity.

"Onyway, one thing led tae another and ah tumbled out of the Big Tree about four hours later thinkin' if ah could just make it to the horse and cairt, Tam could find our way home.

"Afore ah reached the corner ah could hear the commotion down Hozier Street. Must be a fight outside the Catholic Chapel, ah thought. Must be one of they Orange boys scrapping with the Catholics. Do I really want to get mixed up in that? ah says tae maself. But ma brain didn't have a ready answer. Ah pushed maself aff the lamppost and made a zigzag line across to where I'd left the cairt.

"Something was wrong! Where was Tam? Ah looked up the close—nothin' there. Then ah saw the cairt restin' on its shafts. The smithy was closed up; Davy had gone home for his tea. It wasn't like Davy to leave a job unfinished. Ah expected to find Tam standing docile by the cairt, waiting for me ... or even hitched if Davy had taken the time or the bother. But, no.

"Right then, two wee lads ran past and nearly knocked me over. They were callin' to anyone who wanted to hear. 'There's a horse in the Chapel. There's a big horse in the Chapel.'

"Ah came out of the daze as it dawned on me. IT MUST BE TAM. Ah threw back ma shouthers and walked in the direction of St. Mary's towards the awful yelling ah could hear.

"'There he is,' says Mrs. Riley who was headed to the Big Tree Bar to extricate her husband. She had a baby wrapped in a shawl and the other arm free to push two wide-eyed weans ahead of her.

"'He's drunk, Father,' she says tae the priest. Which wasn't true.

"'Do you know this man, Missus Riley? Is this the owner of that wild animal?' says the priest.

"''Tis,' she says, glowerin' at me.

"'Have you lot taken my horse?' says I, figuring a frontal attack might work better.

"'Taken your horse, is it?' says the priest all red-faced, practically spittin' out the words. 'He's drunk every bit of the Holy Watter and tomorrow is the Sabbath. And, by the by, it's not goin' to increase his chances any more than yours of getting into heaven.'

"'Do ye tell me?' I says, tryin' tae keep a straight face.

"The last shilling's worth of drinks must have kicked in at that moment and ah collapsed on the street. Last I heard was Father Flanagan sayin', 'Frances Dougherty, run down to Whifflet Street and find the constable.'

"Ah gave Tam a guid talkin' to after that debacle. Says I, 'Tam, if ye're goin' tae get religion, ye cannae be makin' arbitrary decisions aboot it, wi' me bein' an Orangeman an' all.'"

Grandpa re-lit his pipe. "Did ah ever tell ye about Mike Rafferty getting thrown out of The Big Tree Bar?

Showdown at the Big Tree Bar

He was a care-defying blade as ever Bacchus listed
                                              ... Robert Burns

That Sunday when we went to Grandpa's, Grandma had left to go up to the Salvation Army Hall for the afternoon meeting. Being a former Salvation Army officer herself, she was much in demand for her impassioned prayers that were long enough to satisfy the Lord and the congregation.

We had Grandpa all to ourselves, my three wee brothers and me, and we were settled in for a story. The stories that could be told when Grandma wasn't present had a different flavour that we were old enough to appreciate.

"Did I tell you about the fight my faither, Wullie, got into at the Big Tree Bar?"

"No," four eager voices chorused.

"Aye. It was as hot a night in early July as anyone could remember, and he had the thirst on him still. It was a bad time for Mike Rafferty, the biggest Irishman in the Whifflet, to decide to break his own rule and come in to the Big Tree Bar for a quick pint. With the Orange walk only a week away, the Billy Boys were gearin' up."

Things hadn't changed that much since Grandpa was a youngster at the turn of the century. Even now in 1950 the mining village of Whifflet was divided between Irishmen and Scots, or Catholics and Protestants, and the only time the two crossed paths was down the pit or at a Saturday night brawl. The sectarian sentiment reached fever pitch as "The Glorious Twelfth" approached and the Orangemen geared up for their annual parade. We knew what Grandpa was talking about.

He had told this story so many times, it had the feel of a mythical tale, and he told it almost formally, as though he were reading it, occasionally raising his head to bring the next page into view in his mind's eye.

"Aye. The bar was full of Orangemen, and it was getting late. The Orange songs they were singing with heartfelt melancholy dwindled away to silence when he kicked open the double doors, and Big Mike, in his dark jacket and slouched bunnet, stood silhouetted against the light of the street lamp that twinkled behind him. Three days of beard framed his wicked grin.

"Mike courted trouble. He surveyed the smoky room then swaggered up to the bar where ma faither was holding forth, in a loud voice, on the "Irish Problem," unaware of Mike's grand entrance.

"Faither was a respected leader of the Orange Lodge. He aye rode the big white horse in the parade. He had some opinions and was speakin' out that 'they' (meanin' the Irish) were not only responsible for the recent layoffs but they had probably brought the cholera over with them, too.

"Mike threw down a shilling, clapped his hand on top of it, and demanded, 'What does a daicent fella have to do tae get a pint o' yer piss, barkeep?'

"'Is it piss ye want, Rafferty?' Faither challenged him, drawing himself up to his full height, but the big Irishman still towered over him. Ah wis sittin' nearby at the time but knew better than to get in the middle o' that," Grandpa clarified for us.

"'In a manner of speaking.' Rafferty looked down at

Faither and casually pushed the skip of his dusty cap back with two fingers of his right hand, in a cheeky salute. 'You lot would probably call it nectar of the gods, since you've never tasted better. I'll have some of yer nectar, MacDuff or Macleod or whatever your name is, and a pint of piss for this Scotsman.'

"'They prefer to serve Scotsmen in this establishment.' My faither's quiet hissing tone should have warned Mike that his nemesis was on the edge of explosion. Ah thought of nippin' outside for Uncle Sandy, who was a polisman, but I didn't want to miss any of the action.

"'If there's room in the jug, throw a wee Scotsman in, too. I'll try it.' Says Big Mike, real cheeky-like, considering he was seriously outnumbered.

"The rest of the crowd started to move back, and remained quiet and attentive as the entertainment took centre stage.

"Mike had drunk enough at the other end of town to be more reckless than usual. 'Are you not the puny wee fella that rides the horse in that King Billy parade?' He cocked an eye at Faither, who bristled.

"'I watched that last year from me auntie's window on Hozier Street. Can I ask ye a question ... about the music you were playing and the interesting accompaniment?'

"Faither was temporarily disarmed by the Irishman's interest.

"'Was that you or the horse that farted?'

We exploded in merriment. At that age it was our favourite type of joke. Grandfather used the time to absorb the approval and clear his throat and land a good one right in the centre of the spittoon.

"Faither's first punch almost landed on the big man's jaw, but Mike's nimble dodge caused the right-handed swing to miss its mark and carry my old man in a complete circle. Mike's return punch sent Faither staggering on already uncertain feet. He circled around a couple more times looking for something or someone to break his fall, but the crowd had cleared a place in the centre of the room and we were ranged against the walls. Faither lost his footing and crashed headfirst into the spittoon by the door. He lay there, very still, a surprised look on his face, his arms wrapped around the shiny brass container.

"It was over in the twinkling of an eye. While we waited to see if Faither could make it up for another round, Mike quaffed his beer and headed for the big red doors.

"He says, 'Me faither, back in County Armagh, used to have a couple of Orangemen fur breakfast when the hens weren't laying well. Said they gave him heartburn even when he scrambled them first ... the Orangemen not the eggs.' His grin showed the gaps of missing teeth he'd lost in other skirmishes.

"That Irishman reached the door and spat a direct shot at the polished spittoon, barely missing Faither's head, then he was out the door without a backward glance.

"Wee daft Angus says tae me, 'Did ye see that, Rab? Do ye think he meant tae splash yer faither in his face?'

"'Naw,'" says I. "'If he'd meant tae, he'd have hit him between the eyes. Big Mike was the best shot in Ireland.' Everybody knew that.

"'But this isn't Ireland, Rab.' Angus says.

"Ah followed Mike out. He was halfway up Whifflet Street when the constable hailed him.

"'Is that you, Mick?' Uncle Sandy had overheard the whole how-do-ye-do from under the lamppost at the corner, just outside the bar. He had, of course, been rootin' for the other fella. He could see from this big man that his brother Wullie had been seriously outweighed.

"'Mike Rafferty, your honour," he replies, unwilling to let the insult in the nickname "Mick," used to denote any Irishman, be ignored.

"'Aye, whatever ... was you the one down at the Big Tree raisin' hell?'

"'I did go into that filthy establishment for a small libation,' he says.

"'Big, fancy wurrds fur a navvy.'

"'Thank you, yer honour. I learned the English without the distinct disadvantage of British schooling. A hindrance that affects most of the ignorant Protestants around this inhospitable town.'

Uncle Sandy told us this afterwards. You could tell he admired the Irishman's brash courage.

"Yon Mike wis afraid of nobody.

"'You better come along wi' me. I have some Scottish hospitality for ye,' says Uncle Sandy. 'Another week or two in the jail should bring yer swalt heid down tae size.'

"'I assure you, constable, my head is not swollen. That puny King Billy stand-in never landed a daicent blow.'

"'So ye admit ye beat up a man in the pub without provocation?'

"'Yer wee brother wis askin' fur it,' says Mike."

After the appropriate time for appreciation of the story, Grandpa said, "Did ah ever tell ye the one aboot the Hielanman?"

But mark the Rustic, haggis fed,
The trembling earth resounds his tread.
Clap in his walie nieve a blade,
He'll mak it whissle;
An' legs an' arms, an' heads will sned,
Like taps o' thrissle.

… Robert Burns

Scottish Soul Food

Recipe idea: Haggis Balls.

First: trap your haggis.
   (If you are unsuccessful at this, go to your nearest Scottish butcher and get a genuine haggis.)
   Now, assuming the haggis got free and you're having to use one from the butcher, proceed.

Ingredients:

Haggis
1 or 2 eggs separated (depending on the size of the haggis)
Beaten yolks are mixed in a bowl with the haggis to a soft consistency
Add a wee tot of usquebae (whisky)
Breadcrumbs
Form the haggis and egg mixture and the usquebae into balls then roll them in beaten egg white
Roll the balls in breadcrumbs
Deep fry to a crisp, golden brown

Word of warning: my friend Anne in Vancouver, Canada offered these at a Hogmanay party. One lady (not Scottish) complimented her on the "Meat Balls."
"What's in them?" she sez.
"Haggis," sez Anne proudly.
The nice lady spat it out on the floor.

So I suggest you tell the uninitiated up front what is in the delicious dish or lie about it after the fact.

Colin's Mince and Tatties

In case you think this is attributed to a Scotsman in error, I have it on good authority that the one thing a majority of Scotsmen are not ashamed to be caught in the kitchen preparing is: Mince and Tatties. I've heard tell they'll put together a good pot of soup too but nae fancy cakes or shortbread or trifle or onything wi' a foreign sounding name.

"Mince and Tatties" is otherwise known as Scottish Soul Food. (Ask Colin)

Recipe:

First tak' a pun a mince.
Dice an onion (better still have the wife do it—no good tae have her see ye greetin').
Brown in pan—stir ferociously so it disnae stick.
Add water to cover. And salt and pepper to taste. Carrots and frozen peas optional. If yer on some kind of health kick.
Bile hauf a hoor.
Add a squish of HP sauce (secret ingredient).
Meanwhile peel hauf a stane of tatties an' neeps too if ye have them.

May be served in chunks or mashed if ye want to be fancy.

The Scottish National Party aka Hogmanay

Hogmanay: A Scottish New Year

I miss Scotland most on Hogmanay, the last night of the year.

When I was a recent immigrant to the USA I became enthusiastically involved in the extravagant preparations for Christmas that seemed to start when summer was barely over. It was something new, even exotic. Christmas was never a major holiday in Scotland. It was a religious event that included an extra church service, a few traditional carols, and dinner at Granny's, after which we got ready for the big event, Hogmanay, leading to Ne'erday, New Year's Day.

Post World War II Scotland was a time of transition as far as the "Holidays" as a concept was concerned. I think the term used was "the turn o' the year," referring to Christmas and New Year. The traditional Scottish focus on Hogmanay was just beginning to share the spotlight with the secular aspects of the Christmas festivity.

HOG-ma-nay! (The meaning of the word is lost in antiquity.) The night before New Year's Day was still the big celebration. Enough information about tinsel-covered Christmas trees and Santa Claus had filtered through from

England and from Hollywood's over-the-top technicolor movie representations to raise our youthful expectations of unlimited brightly wrapped gifts arriving on Christmas Day. It made me, as a child, expect more fanfare about Christmas than my parents were accustomed to or willing to extend. But, to give them their due, they tried to adopt the spirit, and there was always at least one wrapped present from Santa and the inevitable hand-knit socks from Granny, at least one pair for each of her ten grandchildren. And in last year's sock, hanging over the fireplace sporting some careful darning, were some of our favourite sweeties and an orange covering the top of it. Don't get me wrong, we appreciated the warm wool socks, and we could more easily find a matching pair ... at least for a while.

Some Santa gifts were spectacular. One year I got a doll from Canada. During the scarcities of the post-war period these dolls, with the china head, were impossible to find ... and I got one. It was a treasure.

But Christmas at that time in Scotland was primarily a religious holiday and basically it was simply "the week before Ne'erday."

The big event was coming, and preparations had to be made. In addition to the baking of Black Bun, Dundee Cake, and Shortbread, the round of cleaning was relentless. Rooms were painted or wallpapered; new curtains purchased; bills paid up to date. One had to go into the New Year with a clean slate. And last thing before midnight on Hogmanay the ashes were cleaned out of the fireplace.

Of course, that is not what I miss. I had only a few adult New Years in Scotland before I left for America. What I remember are the joyful, carefree celebrations, not the scrupulous cleaning.

I miss Hogmanay, that night of the year when Scotland really shows off her generosity and open-heartedness. Everybody's house is your house; you are welcome wherever you go.

I remember "First-Footin'," which is a traditional all-night affair. Folks go from house to house enjoying a wee tot 'o whisky and the hostess's home-baked treats. At least one in the party of revellers must be a tall, dark-haired person assigned to cross over the threshold first after midnight carrying a gift (or a piece of coal could be substituted). To bring good luck to the family all year, they mustnae be empty-handed. I miss the rowdy singing of the old songs, meeting only friends on that night, some old and some new. The whole country became a village and you were its child.

For years after I emigrated, I cried every Hogmanay. When the bells rang at midnight and the people greeted each other, I found a quiet place to express my private grief. Tears that no one could have understood. Tears I barely understood myself; the tears of the homesick traveller.

One year, when my daughter was only two, I couldn't stand it any longer and packed her up and braved the hectic traffic of expatriates descending on Scotland. We flew out of Montreal that year and returned to Coatbridge in time for New Year. My parents were only too happy to have their first grandchild for a Hogmanay visit to spoil for a while. Meantime, I joined my party-going brothers.

I'd like to think I'm older and wiser now. At least, I know I'm older. Partying all night doesn't have the same appeal!

But there is something about the essence of Hogmanay that is truly Scottish. The riotous sharing of stories, songs, the open houses, and the generosity.

The Scots visualized a clean slate and welcomed a new beginning and showed the bravery, even in tough times, to expect that a New Year could and would offer a fresh start.

By emptying out the ashes of the old fires our forebears invited good fortune to visit the cleaned hearth.

May the New Year lead you to a safe haven, an open door, a good laugh, an open mind, the hand of friendship, and the dialogue of peace.

LUMPY PORRIDGE

Robert Burns says it best:

Then let us pray that come what may,
As come it will for a' that;
That sense and worth o'er all the earth,
May bear the gree, and a' that,
For a' that and a' that,
It's coming yet, for a' that,
That man to man the world o'er
Shall brothers be for a' that.

Och, I think I'm goin' tae cry!

My First Hogmanay

The first time a Scot gets to welcome in the New Year as an adult must be one of those memorable "Firsts," like First Kiss, First Love, First Flight or First (you fill in the blank). At least, it seemed so to me at fifteen. Hey! It's Scottish Party Night.

The local Wee Free Church that my born-again Mum made us attend faithfully had a well-earned reputation for sticking to the straight and narrow. It gave my poor old Mum the awesome responsibility of making sure her errant daughter did not commit even the slightest sin.

The list of restrictions was long, even more detailed than the Scottish standards of the time, and made her job very difficult. No dancing, singing popular songs, going to the pictures, or wearing lipstick, to name a few of the ones I thought cramped my style unnecessarily. The congregation was "wee," but as a teenager it didn't seem very "free" to me, and they diligently kept an eye on me and my pals when our Mums weren't there to do it.

But the Hogmanay I turned fifteen, it all changed. I discovered Freedom.

"Aye, ye can go out with your pals," Mum said.

"And what time do I need to be home?"

"Och, it's Hogmanay, Harriet. Let the lassie have a bit of fun." This from my favourite uncle who'd probably had a wee dram on his way over to our strictly teetotal house.

I could see Mum was in a good mood. After all, it's the greatest holiday on the Scottish calendar. Our house would be open for a First-Footer and visited by friends and neighbours till the wee hours. Nobody sleeps on New Year's Eve. It's a law, I think.

I hurried out the door before she changed her mind, my thoughts firmly focused on doing a wee bit singin' and hoochin' and dancin,' and maybe hear the skirl o' the bagpipes along the way. I stopped only to retrieve my contraband lipstick, stashed behind the aspidistra in the hall. I ran awkwardly in my new high heels to catch the bus for a prearranged rendezvous with a group of age-mates from the church, who were equally excited about trying out new freedoms.

Och, it was the greatest night!

A crisp cold night, no rain, full moon; that wee nippy breeze just gave us more pep, and sure enough, at a safe distance came the unmistakable tuning up of a lone piper. We lengthened our stride to fit "Scotland the Brave."

A night to bring in Ne'erday in style. No drinking, mind you. That would have been way beyond bad and we didn't need it anyway; we were too full of youthful exuberance. In the back of my mind I would have heard Mum intoning, "The taste of whusky has never passed ma lips."

There were about ten of us rarin' to go, arms linked, dancing from one house to the next, singing "Scots, wha ha'e", " Gin a body", "Ah belang tae Glesca", and other classics, till we were hoarse.

Big Jimmy with the dark curly hair was appointed the "First-Footer" to go to each door and knock and be the first one to cross the threshold after midnight to bring them good luck for the New Year. He couldn't go in empty-handed, of course, so he carried a lump of coal. It was the best we could manage. At each house we left we took a chunk out of the coal bin and passed it on to the next host. So it sort of evened out. At the houses of our pals who had to stay home and didn't achieve Freedom that night, we presented our gift, which they added to the already roaring fire. We sat around for songs and feasting, then on to the next house.

The last stop was my Granny's. When we emerged from her close, (a covered alley between buildings) creating a deafening din, she was returning from taking the ashes out to the bin. She donned a clean apron, and led us through her newly whitewashed kitchen to her recently re-papered living room. Every inch of that house had been scrubbed, cleaned, and polished to perfection in the previous week. The smell of carbolic soap and fresh paint was aired out of the house which now welcomed us with the fragrance of home baking as only she could produce it.

Freshly baked scones steamed near the oven. Traditional black bun soaked for a respectable number of weeks in whisky evaporated its fragrance into the tiny kitchen. After a big Scottish welcome and many "Happy New Years," we thirsty balladeers quaffed several big pots of tea and attacked the best shortbread and black bun this side of paradise, spread out on Granny's crisp lace cloth. We each got a wee tumbler of her homemade elderberry wine, which she swore was non-alcoholic, "but dinnae mention it to yer mither." We raised our glasses and drank to her, "Lang may yer lum reek."

Oh, and for all you Scots around the world, who gather together to bring in the New Year, a toast:

Here's tae us wha's like us.

LUMPY PORRIDGE

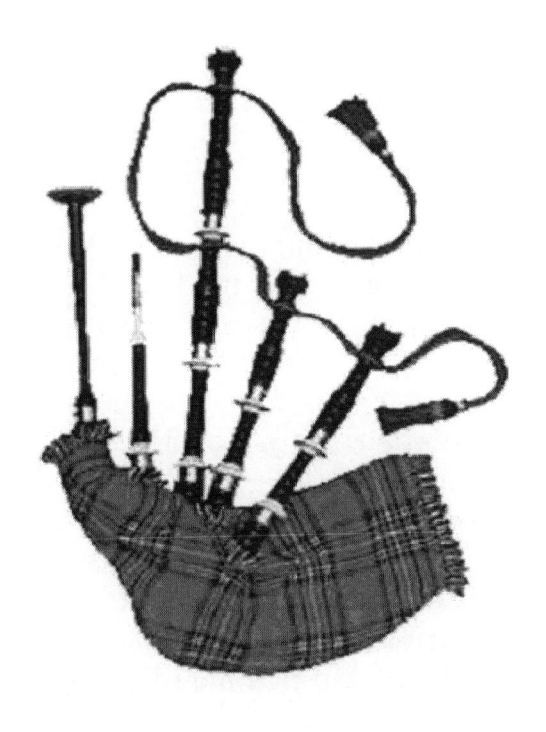

New Year Resolutions

In November and December you take a hard look at yourself. You've gained weight; you're drinking too much; you haven't exercised for months (your favourite chair is permanently moulded to the shape of your expanding rear end); you forgot to call your mother again this weekend. Add your own sins to this list.

It is hard to live with all the guilt. That's why we have New Year's resolutions. Before New Year you can pat your wayward self on the back and say, "Come January first I'll stop smoking, go on a diet, clean out the garage, quit yelling at the kids, etc."

In your vivid imagination it is a fait accompli or a done deal, as they say in the U.S. You will start on January One ... promise.

Nae bother at a'. Now you can hunker down in your easy chair, light a fag, ask the wife while she's up to get you a cold one, and break open a packet of crisps, confident that you will work off these extra calories in a few weeks. Och aye! That feels great.

To feel better yet, you could write up your list of resolutions, type it, or put it into your computer. While ye're at it, why not prioritize and alphabetize it? There ye go.

Problem is, January the first arrives, and you've been out First-Footin' till 5 a.m. This was the day you had planned to walk two miles. Jings! Getting to the fridge for a glass of orange juice is about all you can handle without triggering the groaning pain in yer heid. Gie's a brek!

In the fervour of creating your resolutions you should've agreed with yourself to begin mending your ways January second. Maybe you can just give up the ciggies for a couple of days without blowing a gasket. That would be a start.

But get halfway into January and the bills start coming in, the weather is brutal, and the party's over. What happens then?

The small voice whispers "Och, one wee puff isnae goin' tae hurt ye."

Or "It's gie cold tae walk today. Do it tomorrow."

I can hear you. But failure isn't an option.

Maybe you've been lucky and lost your list of resolutions or your computer developed a glitch. Your resolves have evaporated into cyberspace.

Postponement is, of course, one choice. After all, the refrigerator is still full of treats. What a waste to throw out the leftover turkey dressing or the apple pie your non-smoking teetotal sister-in-law with the perfect figure contributed to the party. January is a bad month to put yourself under additional stress, what with the bills coming in and fuel just went up.

It's cold, the nights are long. You could put it off till February or at least till after the Burns' supper.

Negotiation is another alternative. You could modify your list.

Yes. Great idea. How about a modified list?

You'll "cut down" on smoking.

You'll just walk down to the corner. A good start.

You'll sign up for the gym when they offer that special.

The possibilities are endless.

But (and here is the escape clause) ... why bother with all that work and effort!

This year I resolved NOT to make any resolutions.

It's February. So far it's workin' smashin'.

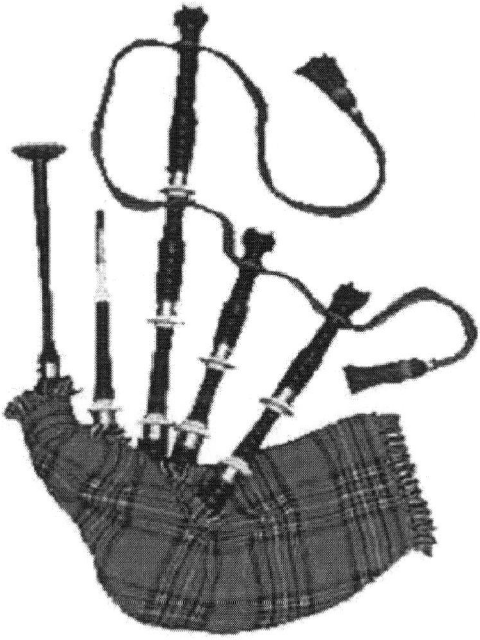

For auld lang syne, my dear.
For auld lang syne,
We' ll tak a cup o' kindness yet,
For auld lang syne.

Robert Burns

New Year in a Highland Croft~1860

From the novel *My Blood Is Royal*
by Joyce Milne D'Auria

And there's a hand, my trusty fiere,
And gie's a hand o' thine:
And we'll tak' a right guid-willie-waught,
For auld syne.

Robert Burns

For sixteen-year-old Lizzie, the best thing about winter was the celebration that started on Hogmanay, New Year's Eve, and lasted all night till New Year's Day. Hog-man-NAY! She said it over and over again to herself. The biggest celebration on the Scottish calendar started on Hogmanay, New Year's Eve, and lasted all night till Ne'erday, New Year's Day.

The white blanket that was banked several feet up to the only window, helped to keep the stone croft warm; as did the animals her father and brother brought into the adjacent byre for the winter.

Lizzie, her sister Annie, and her mother Flora, had been baking and cleaning for weeks, tripping over the twins and wee Gregor in the confined space of the fire room.

On the last day of the old year everyone took turns bathing in the huge wooden tub in front of the peat fire, then dressed in their finest and waited for Hogmanay.

With fresh new snow on the ground, a visitor after midnight would be sure to know if he was the first. He must be tall and dark and carry a gift. It was an old tradition, and such a First-Footer would bring luck to the family all year.

Leaning over the deep window-shelf, Lizzie admired the blanket of snow sparkling in the late December moonlight. Fresh snow had fallen on this last day of December; the Scottish Highlands had on a brand-new coat to welcome 1860. A path had been dug to the outhouse and the gate.

On other years the MacGregors had gone out in the closeknit clachan, calling on all their neighbours in the hamlet. They would be hosts this year and see who visited. Who would be the first to step over the threshold after midnight? Who would claim the honour of "First-Footin'?" Probably the Campbells from next door. Would Jock Campbell accompany his family or go out with some of his mates? Lizzie lay awake nights thinking about his shy smile.

Excitement had been growing in Lizzie since Ma started the cooking weeks before. Lizzie saw her reach deep into her dresser for the jars of currants, Muscat raisins, almonds, and ginger she hoarded to bake the black bun. With the right amount of whisky added, the mixture was poured into a deep pastry shell, covered with more pastry, and baked for three hours in a heavy cauldron buried in the peat fire, then stored for at least four weeks to develop the rich flavour.

Lizzie churned extra butter for the shortbread and, under Ma's eagle eye, kneaded it into their finest milled wheat flour and sugar and baked it to a honey gold colour, then cut the circles into triangles, dusted them with sugar, and placed them in a tin for the big day.

For a week before Hogmanay there was a frenzy of activity. The men cleaned out the byre. Lizzie and her sister Annie swept and scrubbed the flagstone floor. Though Annie was fifteen, only two years younger, Lizzie had to nag her to do her part. Ma's girth made it impossible for her to do heavy labour. Her mother rested often. Her time was near. It would be a January baby. Winter babies had a tougher time surviving in the damp cold of the Highlands.

After dark on Hogmanay they straightened out the room; took turns washing themselves in the big tub by the fire, and put on their best clothes. Flora added a lace collar, which had been her mother's, to the neck of her fine grey wool dress. Lizzie combed her hair and tied it up with a green ribbon and groomed Annie's hair. The girls donned with pride the brightly coloured hand-knitted shawls their mother had made for a New Year's gift.

Then they waited.

Lizzie heard John Campbell first, coming round the hill. He'd been at some other parties before this by the sound of him. He sang an old Covenanter's song, joined lustily by his grown sons.

Lizzie checked herself in the mirror and straightened her ribbon; in the light of the paraffin lamp she could tell her cheeks were pink from excitement.

"Och, I hope Jock brought his fiddle," she said to Annie.

"Why? Are you going to sing again?" Annie had no idea she couldn't carry a tune, and couldn't understand why she was never invited to sing.

"We'll all sing," said her mother so Annie wouldn't take a huff and try to spoil the evening.

"Are ye there, MacGregor? We're coming in," yelled John.

"Sweesht, John. Ye'll waken the bairns," said Nellie Campbell in a stage whisper.

"Ach, woman, what kind of Scot, young or old, sleeps on Hogmanay. Open the door, MacGregor. I have a wee dram for ye."

"Comin', John. Comin' right away." Pa never answered the door, that was a job for one of the women, but tonight he forgot himself in his enthusiasm.

LUMPY PORRIDGE

Over the noise of the Hogmanay greetings and the wind howling down the glen she heard the Robertsons' piper across Loch Rannoch playing "Auld Lang Syne."

Aleck Campbell, the oldest, tallest brother, led the parade across the threshold. Aleck had the darkest hair of the sandy-haired family.

Nellie called to him, "Aleck, carry this in."

"What for, Ma?"

"Ye can't walk in empty-handed. Ye'll bring the MacGregors bad luck, ye glaikit big tattiebogle."

His brothers laughed at the tall fellow getting lessons in Highland etiquette from his diminutive mother. She pushed towards him the fragrant pot of mutton stew she had made. He stumbled and blushed to be seen carrying it in front of so many men, yet to walk in empty-handed would have been an affront to his host and hostess.

The youngest Campbell, his father's namesake and the object of Lizzie's daydreams, was dubbed 'Jock' to avoid confusion. He entered last. Tonight he walked past her with only a slight nod in her direction and headed for a place on the bench next to her brother Charlie. After they filed in they arranged themselves by the fire—women on one side, men on the other. Bairns, down to the youngest, wide awake, jockeyed to get close to their favourite adult on a lap or a stool.

"Here's a bottle of the best, Flora." Jock's father said.

"Aye, I'll get glasses out right away, John."

Nellie helped Flora bring out the food. Lizzie put some more peat on the fire, while her father, Charlie, John Campbell, and his three boys sipped on the whisky.

Flora retrieved a bottle of her own homemade elderberry wine from her kist and poured two glasses. She slid one across the sideboard to Nellie, who favoured her with a wide grin that revealed several gaps in her teeth—about one for each nine-month it took to birth these braw big sons.

"Not too much, Flora." But she accepted the full glass

with a girlish giggle.

"Here's a drink to those we miss—a toast to the old ones—gone but not forgotten," John said solemnly with his best ceremonial intonation.

He took a long draught from the cup, exhaled, and wiped his mouth with the back of his hand. "Remember yer father, Rab?" John sighed and raised his glass to his friend. "A finer man ye'd never meet than old Gregor. When yer mother caught a fever and died he, no six weeks later, joins her." John heaved an audible sigh.

"Funny how that happens with auld folk; they both go thegither. I often wondered if they have an appointment at the same time with the Almighty."

Lizzie feared this memory might disturb her father and stole a glance at Robert in the pensive silence. Was it too soon to joke about Auld Gregor?

"My father was probably late for that appointment too. He was never in time for anything in his life."

It was all right, Lizzie thought. We can laugh about it now.

"There was a man could tell a yarn though," John went on. "Remember the one about the MacGregors?"

"What MacGregors? We're all MacGregors one way or another in this glen."

Her father's voice was sharp, but she knew it wasn't directed at John. It was a sore point with the folks in Glen Orchy and Rannoch Moor, many of whom claimed ancestry to the outlawed Clan MacGregor but had to adopt different names due to a quirk of history.

Pa tried to appease him by offering a toast. "Raise a glass to the MacGregors wherever they are, or whatever they're called—in Bonnie Scotland or roaming in foreign lands."

"To the MacGregors." They solemnly raised their glasses.

"Tell old Gregor's yarn, John." Nellie said.

Lizzie settled down on a milking stool near the fire for

the storytelling, and took Gregor on her lap. The fire lit the faces of the expectant gathering. Lizzie's eyes met Jock's; his face seemed redder than the others. He quickly turned his head and said something to Annie that made her simper. Could it be that Jock was taken with Annie? She dismissed the thought.

Jock's father signalled to his wife to refresh his drink.

"Seems these English bastards—"

"You mind yer tongue, John Campbell," Mrs. Campbell warned.

"What would you call them, lass? All right, then. These English devils were Redcoats on patrol near Loch Rannoch. Hunting down Prince Charlie's men, they were. Searching for Black Duncan Cameron, who was from hereabouts. When the patrol got to Schiehallion, they saw a Highland man up on the hill cursing them out in the Gaelic. A private and a corporal volunteered to go up the hill and capture him or kill him. Off they went on their horses.

"In the valley down below, they could hear the sound of a skirmish up there; then all was quiet." John dropped his voice to a whisper.

"The Highland man appeared and hefted his kilt over his shoulders and gave them a good view of his backside. Yon English commander wasn't amused, so he sent a troop of soldiers up the side of the hill and waited. Sure enough they heard the sound of battle and some bloodcurdling screams ... then all was quiet.

"The Highland man came to the top of the hill. He was missing his Glengarry bunnet and a bit dishevelled over all, but he was able to give the officer a two-finger salute he recognized well enough even from the distance. Was that officer mad! He ordered the attack, and with the bugle blasting, the whole battalion galloped up the hill. As they neared the top, the wee English corporal comes running out waving his arms frantic-like. 'Git back. Git back,' he yells. 'It's a trap—there's two of them.'"

When the laughter subsided after hours of stories, Jock's mother said, "Enough of yer tall tales, John Campbell. Let's have some music."

"C'mon Jock, lad, give us a tune on the fiddle," John Campbell called to his son.

Lizzie watched Jock take out of its case the ancient instrument he had inherited from his grandfather and tune it. She helped Mrs. Campbell and mother get out the sweetmeats and spread them on the sideboard and prepared to make a pot of tea.

The men feasted on black bun and shortbread while he played on his fiddle, "Flora MacDonald's Lament." Lizzie recognized it right away and appreciated that he had learned it to honour her mother.

Flora gave a little curtsy. "Thank you, Jock. My, yer getting awful good on that instrument. Ye'll be playing next year at the feeing market in Dalmaly."

"Play one Lizzie knows. I'd like fine to hear her sweet voice. She never sings loud enough in church. It's hard to hear her over yon Mary Buchanan's skreiching," said Jock's father. He had no affection for the laird's spoiled daughter. "Did ye hear yon woman at the Christmas Eve service? Och, I'd sooner listen to ten bagpipes in a byre full of chickens."

Pa smiled and said, "Now, John, there's nothing worse than a woman with a swollen head."

"Och, the lassie's head's not swollen. Lizzie's got talent, let her enjoy it. Let's all enjoy it."

Lizzie took a deep breath, cocked her eye towards her father as though to dare him to deny the compliment.

With that introduction, Lizzie stood up beside Jock, who moved away from her as far as he could in the small room. Lizzie stared at him, bewildered, then noticed the reaction of the wise mothers, who nudged each other and hid smiles. Hmmm!

"I'd like to sing 'Comin' Thru the Rye,'" she announced with more assurance than she felt. She threw her shoulders back, took a deep breath, and tried to imagine herself out in the field walking alone and singing with confidence. She tried to forget she was in these cramped quarters with everyone staring at her, and Jock Campbell with that silly look on his face and it almost the same colour as the fire. What is the matter with him? She thought. Maybe he can't play it. Och! Everybody knows that one surely.

Jock gave her a few bars of introduction and her clear voice rang out over his perfect accompaniment. He must have been practicing, she thought, and gave him a nod of appreciation when the assembled gathering, except for Annie, broke into applause, then fell on the rich food spread out before them.

The clootie dumpling simmering in the pot was fished out and its cloth cover removed. Her wee brother cried out in delight when he found a paper wrapped ha'penny in the pudding. Lizzie had found a slice for him that contained the prize. The rich fragrant pudding smelled of cinnamon and nutmeg and was bursting with raisins. It was presented, steaming hot, on Flora's precious blue and white Prestonpans platter she usually kept in her kist for safety.

She saw Nellie Campbell casting an envious eye on the platter. The rest of the party was only interested in seeing its contents divided and shared.

"Time for a wee bit more of the uisge beatha, the aqua vita, as the laird might call it." John poured whisky into the traditional quaich, a silver, two-handled cup Flora set out beside the dumpling.

"Slainte mhath!" He raised the cup with the traditional Gaelic toast then passed it to Robert.

"Aye, John, to your good health too."

Flora sliced the dumpling and served generous portions, first to the men and boys, then to Nellie and the girls, and served herself a piece last.

"A toast," said Robert. "To the Auld Laird. May he live long."

"Slainte! To the Auld Laird." Everyone raised a glass to toast the landlord. The older ones had whisky; the younger ones got a wee taste of elderberry wine for a treat.

"Heard tell he's not that well. Getting worse by the day. Terrible gout in his foot, they say." Jock's mother delivered this inside information with an air of importance.

"Living with those women he has to live with, he probably has pains in other places too," John tossed back at her.

"Is that a fact?" Aleck stuffed his mouth with dumpling and almost swallowed a ha'penny.

"Mind yer manners," his mother cautioned.

"Time to go to bed now." Her mother shooed the young ones and Annie into the sleeping room amidst sleepy complaints.

Jock leaned across the table while everyone else was engrossed in the gossip about the gentry and whispered. "Lizzie, if ye like we could go up the Aulich hill the next dry day and practice duets with the fiddle."

Lizzie looked at him amazed and wondered if he'd had a drop of the "water of life" himself. But his steady blue gaze never wavered, though his face got redder under her questioning stare.

"I know ye sing up there alone sometimes. I've heard ye when I'm fishing at the burn …" His voice trailed off. He must have known these were Lizzie's private moments.

"I'd like that, Jock." She covered her surprise and delight with a polite, "Thank you," then turned her attention to the story in progress, unable to trust herself to stay locked on his intent look over-long.

The cup was passed again.

Well after midnight and close to morning the singing and storytelling ended, and the Campbells bundled themselves against the blowing snow and took their lanterns to light the way to their croft a few hundred yards round the hill. Chickens fluttered down from their roost in the entryway and the cock crowed lustily.

"Here's a wee kiss for ma dearie," she heard her father say. "Ye did us proud. Yon black bun was better than even my mother made."

This was the highest compliment he could pay.

"It was a grand evening, Rob. The best in the sixteen years we've spent together."

New Year was a time to affirm commitments.

Lizzie crawled onto her straw-filled mattresses for an hour's rest. The New Year had been properly welcomed.

She'd turn sixteen this year. That felt to her to have special significance; how would Jock figure in her life this year?

She remembered his red face. Och, things could never be the same again as when we were children together. She felt different about him.

Very different.

Mair Scottish Wurrds

SKIRL: (def) a scream, a shriek of pain
         (def) of bagpipes, make a shrill sound

This is perhaps why I enjoy my bagpipe music in the open air and not in close quarters.

"Yon Duncan MacTavish upstairs was practicin'
    skirlin' with his chanter till the wee hoors.
Aboot two in the mornin' ah let out a skirl maself.
    There was such a jabbin' pain in ma heid."

To order books:

www.JoyceTheScottishWriter.com
Online from Amazon and Barnes and Noble
on both sides of the pond

About the Author

Born in Lowland Scotland in the industrial town of Coatbridge, Joyce was raised in the post WWII years with three young brothers and a close extended family of aunts, uncles, and cousins living in the same town, and was fortunate enough to get to know two grannies and one story-telling grandpa.

Instead of reading to her youngest brother she would make up stories while he listened enthralled. In this way her storytelling career started early, but growing up intervened, then several years in the family hardware business in Baillieston, on to Nursing School at Glasgow Royal Infirmary, then emigration to the United States, the birth of a daughter, Linda MacIntyre Frame, more schooling, a second career as a counselor, and a move to Florida before she again found time for storytelling. Scotland was her initial inspiration, and the heroic lives of the grannies needed exploring, but, in the process of writing their story, the muse they set in motion led farther afield and a novel, *My Blood Is Royal*, about a highland lass evicted from her home to grapple with the rough 19th century existence in the lowland village of Whifflet. The novel took on a life of its own, and was followed by a sequel, *Billy Boy, Caught Between the Orange and the Green*. Both are set in 19th century Scotland and in North America. Coming in 2016 her latest novel, *Bridge Across Time*, promises something a bit different.

A short story won first prize in Penwomen's Clearwater competition and chapters from her novel *My Blood Is Royal*, won awards in the Cincinnati Celtic Festival and in Florida Writers' Association.

She lives with her husband Paul near Dunedin, Florida. She regularly "crosses the pond" to nourish her Scottish roots.

*For information about
presentations and appearances
and other contact information,
visit the author's web site:*
www.JoyceTheScottishWriter.com

Acknowledgments:

Special thanks go to my fellow travellers in Scotland, Beryl Maclean and Ann Shimmins, who seemed to enjoy trekking around our homeland with me, collecting tidbits for stories.

Gratitude goes to Mein Host James Shimmins, cousin and sometime editor, for the gracious accommodations in Balfron, the yarns we shared around his kitchen table about our family and, of course, for the fish and chips at "The Clachan" in Balloch.

To my Canadian friends Anne and Robin Maclean-Foreman and Colin and Mhairi Hardie who willingly shared their observations about Scotland and growing up there, as well as their experience of being an "expat."

I appreciate their indulgence for being willing to subject themselves to my brand of humour in print knowing that we are laughing with them at the strange human experience we all share—growing older and looking back—called nostalgia.

My appreciation to E. Rose Sabin, author of *A School for Sorcery*, for her editing and guidance in creating this second edition.

And to my daughter, Linda MacIntyre Frame, for her editing in the original *Lumpy Porridge*.

Thanks to the Dunedin, Florida, Writers Group who understood before I did that these memories should be a book.

And, of course, to my long-suffering husband, Paul, who does not know yet about his next trip to Scotland … soon.

Printed in Great Britain
by Amazon